one click

Jeff Bezos and the
Rise of Amazon.com

Richard L. Brandt

PORTFOLIO
PENGUIN

PORTFOLIO PENGUIN

Published by the Penguin Group
Penguin Books Ltd, 80 Strand, London WC2R ORL, England
Penguin Group (USA) Inc., 375 Hudson Street, New York, New York 10014, USA
Penguin Group (Canada), 90 Eglinton Avenue East, Suite 700, Toronto, Ontario, Canada M4P 2Y3
(a division of Pearson Penguin Canada Inc.)
Penguin Ireland, 25 St Stephen's Green, Dublin 2, Ireland (a division of Penguin Books Ltd)
Penguin Group (Australia), 250 Camberwell Road, Camberwell, Victoria 3124, Australia
(a division of Pearson Australia Group Pty)
Penguin Books India Pvt Ltd, 11 Community Centre,
Panchsheel Park, New Delhi – 110 017, India
Penguin Group (NZ), 67 Apollo Drive, Rosedale, Auckland 0632, New Zealand
(a division of Pearson New Zealand Ltd)
Penguin Books (South Africa) (Pty) Ltd, 24 Sturdee Avenue,
Rosebank, Johannesburg 2196, South Africa

Penguin Books Ltd, Registered Offices: 80 Strand, London WC2R ORL, England

www.penguin.com

First published in the United States of America by Portfolio Penguin,
a member of Penguin Group (USA) Inc. 2011
First published in Great Britain by Portfolio Penguin 2011
1

Printed in England by Clays Ltd, St Ives plc

ISBN: 978-0-670-92066-2

www.greenpenguin.co.uk

MIX
Paper from
responsible sources
FSC™ C018179
www.fsc.org

Pengu...
future...
planet...
by the...

To Kim and Leila, for everything.
To Al Zuckerman, for being a great agent.
To Courtney Young, for being a great editor.
And to the memory of Lindy Howe, who always had faith in me.

Contents

1. One Click Is Not Enough   1

2. Portrait of the Entrepreneur as a Young Man   19

3. Jeff Gets a Job   33

4. Jeff Discovers the Internet   43

5. Three Nerds and an Accountant   53

6. How to Build a Better Bookstore   67

7. Growing Pains   81

8. Money to Burn Through   91

9. Growing Up   99

10. Who You Calling a Bookstore?   109

11. The Crash   123

12. Bezos Bets Big on the Kindle   135

13. Is Amazon Killing the Bookstore?   149

14. A Cool Guy with a Funny Laugh   159

15. But What Kind of Manager Is He?   167

16. Head in the Clouds   177

17. Step by Step, Courageously   187

Notes   193

Index   203

one click

Chapter 1

One Click Is Not Enough

To be Earth's most customer-centric company where people can find and discover anything they want to buy online.

—Amazon.com Mission Statement

On September 22, 1994, two months after incorporating Amazon.com and ten months before launching the company, Jeff Bezos decided to learn how to sell books. So he took a course on how to start a bookstore, sponsored by the American Booksellers Association. Some forty to fifty aspiring booksellers, from young people starting out to retired couples thinking about a second career, attended the four-day course at the Benson Hotel in Portland. They sat through courses on topics such as bookstore financial operations, customer service, and handling inventory. One of the instructors was Richard Howorth, owner of Square Books in Oxford, Mississippi.

Howorth is a fanatic about customer service (which happens to be the only way to compete with Amazon.com and the chain stores to this day). To emphasize the importance of service, he related the story of his most extreme example of taking care of a customer.

One of the store's managers walked into Howorth's upstairs office to tell him a customer had a complaint. Howorth strolled downstairs to find out what the problem was. The customer angrily told him that she had parked her car in front of the store, and dirt from potted plants on the store's balcony had somehow fallen on her car. So Howorth offered to wash her car for her. They climbed into her car and drove to a service station with a car wash. But the service station was closed for repairs. She became more irate. Howorth then suggested they drive to his house, where he collected a bucket, soap, and a hose and washed the car himself.

As she drove him back to the store, her attitude changed. She became downright pleasant. In fact, she came back to the store later that afternoon and bought a bunch of books.

Bezos later told an executive at the American Booksellers Association that he was impressed with the story and was determined to make customer service "the cornerstone of Amazon.com." Bezos considered it his most important weapon. "We know that if we can keep our competitors focused on us, while we stay focused on the customer, that ultimately we'll turn out all right," he has said.

Interestingly, Jeff's idea of customer service is different than that held by Howorth, who says personal, face-to-face service with the customer is what's most important. In the Internet game, customer service is mostly done by unemotional computers. "I'll bet *he* hasn't washed a customer's car," Howorth says of Bezos, perhaps with just a touch of bitterness.

In fact, for all his professed dedication to serving the customer,

Bezos's obsession seems to be restricted to building an incredible Web site and to making sure deliveries arrive when promised. It's hard to even find a customer service number on Amazon.com. Bezos wants everything to be done via email. Amazon's customer service started with Bezos himself answering the emails, and by 1999 was manned by five hundred of these "customer care" representatives packed into cubicles and tied to their telephones and email accounts to answer questions from customers.

The people handling these emails are generally overqualified, underpaid people with no experience in bookselling. From the beginning, disaffected academics were popular because they were well-read and could supposedly help find books on a huge variety of topics. They were paid about $10 to $13 an hour, but with the potential of promotions and stock options dangled before their glazed eyes.

Not everyone found Nirvana in this environment. Richard Howard, for example, has a master's degree in literature but decided to take the entry-level customer care job at Amazon in 1998 with hopes of moving into Editorial, where he could write reviews of books. What he found was a work mill with four "Customer Service Tier 1 E-Mail Representatives" to a cubicle. Supervisors listened in on calls to monitor performance, and rated the workers by how many emails or phone calls they could answer per minute.

Howard chronicled his experience for a Seattle newspaper in an article titled "How I 'Escaped' from Amazon.cult."

Human interaction was treated almost as a necessary evil. Howard was given a "Blurb Index," a list of hundreds of short, canned answers to cover virtually any question a customer might ask, which he felt were designed to create "a blandly conventional zone of contact between [Amazon's] agents and customers."

When Howard got a call from a customer one day asking how to find a copy of James Michener's *Centennial* because the customer was interested in Civil War–era fiction, Howard suggested Gore Vidal's *Lincoln* as a better alternative—just the type of thing a knowledgeable employee in a good bookstore might do. Howard spent three or four minutes on the call, he said, and was reprimanded by his supervisor. After three and a half weeks on the job he was fired for not being productive enough. He took a contract job at Microsoft instead.

What the starry-eyed customer service representatives with visions of huge stock options found when starting their jobs at Amazon was long hours and options for just one hundred Amazon shares, as long as they performed well for three years. The best could answer a dozen emails a minute. Those who dropped below seven were often fired. *The Washington Post* did an exposé of this "dark" side of Amazon and quoted one customer service rep as saying, "We're supposed to care deeply about customers, provided we can care deeply about them at an incredible rate of speed."

The customer service reps also had to learn the UNIX software system the company used, and had to take a three-week training course at Amazon to learn how everything worked, including how orders for books were submitted, how they were delivered to the warehouse, how they were shelved, how to match orders to the packed books, and how to choose the best shipping method. The most frequent questions came from people who needed help ordering a book on the site or wanted to know where the book they had ordered was.

But Bezos knew he would never be able to offer the kind of service one gets from a physical store staffed by human helpers. "We're never going to have sofas; we're never going to have lattes," he told *BusinessWeek* magazine in June 1997. Where Bezos really managed to shine was in creating a great online experience with very little human interaction with customers. The site had to be simple, fast, and intuitive. It had to offer an unprecedented number of books at the cheapest price possible and deliver them quickly. The whole thing just had to *work* without problems so that people left the site happy. That seems to be enough for most people. "When we do make a customer unhappy at some point," Bezos was later to explain, "these people come out of the woodwork and say, 'Well, actually that wasn't my experience.' Word-of-mouth is very powerful."

That's especially true on the Internet, where word-of-mouth is viral. On the Internet, says Bezos, "Everybody is a publisher." They blog and they email, and they can turn nasty very quickly. Email, he says, "has some magical ability to turn off the politeness gene in the human being . . . you get these very candid pieces of feedback that tell you exactly how you can improve your service. If I walk into a restaurant and am served a bad meal, I just leave; I never go find the chef and grab him by the collar and say, 'You know, you really shouldn't be cooking.'"

But there have been a few occasions when emails and words spread virally through the Internet were intended to grab Bezos by his virtual collar to yell at him. Bezos has not always anticipated what it means to provide great customer service. In the early days, Amazon had a policy of emptying out customers' shopping carts if they remained idle for thirty days. It seemed reasonable at the time to assume the customer wasn't going to buy the items, an assumption that turned out to be wrong. One customer sent an angry email saying that he had spent hours filling the online cart with items he wanted, then suddenly found one day that his basket had been emptied without any warning. In his email, he said it was a stupid policy. The programmers went back to the files in the database and recovered the items for him. They also eliminated the thirty-day deletion practice. "It probably was a stupid policy," Bezos was later to admit in a speech.

Sometimes the company was not able to live up to its promises. In the early days, the overworked staff might miss the promised shipping dates. In order to make up for it, the shipping costs would be refunded whenever a customer complained.

As Amazon grew, Bezos's dedication to doing what's right for the customer began to slip. He often caught hell for it from customers and had to recant. In 1998, reporters discovered that Amazon had started charging publishers $10,000 to feature books on its home page under headings such as "New and Notable" and "Destined for Greatness" with heavy editorial support from Amazon, including a profile of, or interview with, the author.

Bezos reportedly told his staff it was okay to put placement up for bids. "If Publisher X gives us a better deal [on a new title] than Publisher Y," said Bezos, "and we predict that the customer is going to like both of these books equally but there's only a slot to show one, let's show the one where we make more money."

So what's the big deal? After all, bookstores have long accepted payola to give prime real estate in their stores to new titles. But this was Amazon, the company about which Bezos has boasted, "We may be the most customer-obsessed company to ever occupy planet Earth." This was the company that was supposed to always put customers first, offering the best titles to suit their tastes. Who's to say that the customer would "like both of these books equally" when it comes to a choice between one that will make the company extra money and one that won't? That slope is as slippery as an eel in oil.

After the practice hit the press and customers started complaining to Amazon in a barrage of emails, Bezos decided that full disclosure was the best policy. Amazon started posting notices next to prominently placed books when publishers paid for the placement. When that decision was announced, Bezos was sure to point out that Amazon was the only bookseller that made this disclosure. He also promised to refund any books customers had bought on the basis of these recommendations.

Also in 1999, customers began realizing just how much information Amazon was collecting about their book purchases, tastes, and foibles. It came to light after Amazon bought a small online service called PlanetAll, which would cross-reference book sales with people's zip codes and email addresses. Amazon used the information to recommend books to people who the service determined would have similar tastes and interests. Bezos had to do a partial about-face on this one as well, offering a way for buyers to opt out of the data-sharing program. Today, nobody seems to mind—or think about—the fact that Amazon recommends books based on data from others with "similar tastes." The privacy debate has shifted to Google and Facebook, although those companies are probably no bigger offenders than Amazon.

From the beginning, it was very important to Bezos to make people think he *did* belong on the Internet selling things, so he had to make sure he would impress them. The company might send a hardcover book at the paperback price when the softcover version the customer ordered was out of stock. Also, two years after launching, Bezos created an out-of-print division to search for orphan books. Customers were amazed that they could find such books at Amazon, but nowhere else.

Bezos wants to use technology to provide great service to customers. That philosophy resulted in what is perhaps Amazon's most famous—and infamous—patented software program, known as "1-Click ordering."

The 1-Click software was written mostly by a programmer named Peri Hartman, who joined Amazon in 1997. Hartman was given the task of working on the software that would be the interface to the customers, including the ordering system they would use to buy books.

Hartman recalls that, one day over lunch with Bezos and Shel Kaphan, the head of software development, Bezos told them, "We need something to make the ordering system frictionless. We need to make it so the customer can order products with the least amount of effort. They should be able to click on one thing, and it's done."

A simple idea on simplicity, and Hartman took it literally. He set to work creating a program that would require just one click to order a product. (His name appeared first on the patent application, which became patent number US5960411.) The patent filing was titled, innocuously enough, "Method and system for placing a purchase order via a communications network." More telling was the label in an illustrated flow chart in the patent: "Enable Single-Action Ordering."

—

In fact, it is a simple idea. The nineteen-page patent filing is made up mostly of flow chart diagrams that show the sequence of events that enable buyers to place an order with a single click: Retrieve the buyers' identification and payment methods when they first place an order, enter it into the system, and the next time they look up a book, they'll see a 1-Click ordering button on the buyers' pages.

Sound like a no-brainer? That's what Amazon's competitors thought. Many people in technology hate this type of broad patent, known as a "process patent" since it mainly describes the process of doing something that is, well, patently obvious—in this case, reducing to one the number of clicks needed to make a purchase.

That is, however, the kind of attention to detail that has helped make Amazon.com a success. Jeff Bezos will do anything he can think of to make the process of using Amazon.com easier. The genius is that Bezos thought of it first. He knew that doing anything online had to be simple in an age when people were becoming overwhelmed by complicated computers, software, and Internet technology. This, in fact, was a principle that Larry Page and Sergey Brin adopted a couple years later when creating Google. But few competitors have had the sense to follow this rule. Even today, most Web sites seem to be confusing morasses of text, graphics, videos, flashing ads, and a tangled string of links. Amazon.com doesn't match the simplicity of Google's famously spare site, but it is well designed and easy to navigate.

"His general philosophy was to be friendly to customers," recalls Hartman. "The focus should be on the customer, not on the Web site. It's pretty obvious that a simple Web site is easier to use than one with of a bunch of fancy gadgets. He was adamant about that."

His goal was not just to make browsing for books easy, but an enjoyable experience. "People don't just buy books because they need books," he has said. "There are products like that. Pharmaceuticals are that way. Nobody enjoys browsing the Preparation H counter. But people will gladly spend hours in a bookstore, so you have to make the shopping experience fun and engaging."

It didn't require a free online latte to make customers appreciate Amazon.com. In the late 1990s there was so much room for improvement in Web site design that any incremental advancement was like getting an extra bottle of oxygen on a trek to the top of Mount Everest. "To be nine times bigger than your nearest competitor," Jeff explained to *The Washington Post* in 1998, "you actually only have to be 10 percent better." Three years after the site was launched, he said that the majority of his customers came to the site, not because of advertising, but because of positive word-of-mouth.

From the beginning of his company to the present day, Bezos has been fanatical about squeezing out every incremental percentage point of usefulness in Amazon.com. They're often simple things like the 1-Click feature and, later, a one-click button to designate a gift and have it wrapped. He won't wash a customer's car (there are too many customers for Amazon to provide individual attention), but he's happy to implement new policies if they will help all customers. When one elderly woman sent an email to the company saying she loved ordering books from the site but had to wait for her nephew to come over and tear into the difficult-to-open packaging, Bezos had the packaging redesigned to make it easier to open.

These customer services are often met with resistance. When

the site launched, he started allowing customers to review books on the site, positive or negative. People thought he was crazy for allowing negative reviews. It's not exactly something to help sell books, at least not in the short run. But because bad reviews were allowed as well as good, customers learned they could rely on Amazon.com to point them to books that wouldn't disappoint them—at least to a certain extent. Friends and family of authors often help out with reviews on Amazon to help kick-start sales. Negative reviews are usually genuine, unless posted by an author with a competing title.

Very early on, Bezos started adding best-seller lists on Amazon. By 1998, Amazon customers could see where books ranked on any of two thousand different lists. One of Bezos's favorite stories is that of a book called *Endurance*, by Alfred Lansing. It's a real-life adventure tale about polar explorer Ernest Shackleton, whose ship was crushed by an ice floe. He and his twenty-eight men all survived after a six-month trek hiking out of Antarctica. It was originally published in 1956. In 1998, it ended up as one of the top one hundred best-selling books on Amazon. Its popularity, he said, was "strictly fed by these customer reviews." (Today, a paperback version published in 1999 is still being sold on the site, ranking within the top two thousand best sellers on the site, as well as number one in history books about polar regions and number one among travel books about Antarctica.)

And, of course, discounts are a big reason for the company's success. By 1998 he was discounting four hundred thousand best-selling titles and his customer base had grown to 3.1 million people using the site. But he does not use discounts alone to attract customers. By collecting data on which books customers bought and comparing that to books bought by customers with similar tastes, Amazon's computers can recommend books that others may not have found otherwise.

Bezos believes that he can keep improving that technology to outdo recommendations in the best bookstores. In a speech in 1998, he described it as a steadily improving technology:

> So what we think we can do is use advanced technology, like collaborative filtering and other things, to accelerate that discovery process. So that, if today you have a 1-in-1,000 chance when you go in a bookstore of stumbling on something that blows you away, we want to use technology to get to know you as an individual and then make that a 1-in-300 chance. Then a 1-in-100 chance. And then work a few more years on it and make it a 1-in-50 chance and so on and so on. That will create huge value for people. Great merchants have never had the opportunity to understand their customers in a truly individualized way. E-commerce is going to make that possible.

Another feature, added in October 2001, is "Look Inside the Book." Not all publishers or authors like the idea of letting people read some of the book before buying it. Even worse, two years later he added "Search Inside the Book," allowing people to pick out only the topics they're interested in without paying a cent. It's a great research tool for college students, but doesn't bring in revenues for either the publishers or Amazon.com. It does, however, create enormous goodwill and brings people back to the site. Some of them end up buying that book or others on the site.

—

The 1-Click patent, however, created the most controversy, one that lasted for more than a decade. The reason is that anyone else trying to sell anything online is prohibited from adding a one-click purchasing option—unless they want to pay a royalty to Amazon. The patent was written broadly enough that competitors were prevented not only from imitating the code, but from adding a single-click feature at all, regardless of how they made it happen. There are simply not very many ways to add the feature, and none of the approaches are unique enough to avoid violating the patent.

This kind of patent might be compared to filing a patent for a plastic toy that locks out any competitor who might want to make, say, "a disk with a curved edge, which can be thrown long distances by tossing and spinning it." Even the inventor of the Frisbee flying disk, Walter Frederick Morrison, improved on the Frisbie pie pans that were first used for that purpose by describing a specific shape to the curved rim. That shape, called the "Morrison Slope," improved distance and accuracy of the thrown disk. Morrison still managed to make about a million dollars in royalties from his design despite many competitors.

The 1-Click patent was granted by the United States Patent and Trademark Office in September 1999. After it was granted, it attracted enormous derision from those creating retail sites on the Internet, as well as advocates of patent reform. Patents are supposed to be granted only for "non-obvious" inventions. How much thinking does it take to figure out how to cut the ordering process to a single click? Legal experts began referring to it as the "notorious" patent. An article in one law journal described it as "probably the most memorable example of an unoriginal software-patent." Technology book publisher and open-source advocate Tim O'Reilly described that patent as "one more example of an intellectual property milieu gone mad." In an open letter to Bezos, published online, he said that the patent "fails to meet even the most rudimentary tests for novelty and non-obviousness to an expert in the field" and would stifle creativity on the Internet. He asked people to sign a petition to get Bezos to give up the patent.

The legal battle was slow and furious, and wasn't resolved until 2009. In the meantime, Barnes & Noble tried to get around the patent. Amazon owned 1-Click? Well, B&N decided two clicks were almost as good as one. In May 1998 it introduced its own fast checkout system, called "Express Lane," which simply added a second click: After customers clicked on the express purchase button, a second button popped up asking the buyer to click again to confirm the purchase.

Jeff Bezos was not amused—or taken in by the tactic. Three months after his patent was granted, he sued B&N for patent infringement. "We spent thousands of hours to develop our 1-Click process," he said in a press release, "and the reason we have a patent system in this country is to encourage people to take these kinds of risks and make these kinds of investments for customers."

Barnes & Noble fired back with its own press release, insisting that the suit was a "desperate attempt to retaliate for our growing market share" in online bookselling. It didn't specify exactly how fast that share of market was growing. (By 2010, Barnes & Noble was suffering, while Amazon.com is as strong as ever.)

In response to Amazon.com's lawsuit against Barnes & Noble, the Free Software Foundation, an advocacy group that promotes open-source software and is staunchly against software patents, called for a boycott against Amazon.com. That didn't work either.

In December 1999, a district court in Washington State upheld Amazon's patent, issuing a preliminary injunction preventing Barnes & Noble from using Express Lane. The appeal took several years. Finally, in 2002, Barnes & Noble settled the suit with Amazon.com. Although terms were not disclosed, Barnes & Noble was finally able to put its fast purchase method on its site.

Apple Computer took the easy route. In 2000, it licensed the 1-Click patent from Amazon.com, and put the capability on its iTunes store.

Ironically, even Bezos himself now argues against trivial patents. Influenced by O'Reilly, he has traveled with the technology publisher to Washington, D.C., to argue that patent rules should be tightened. The two men even cofounded a Boston company called BountyQuest, which offered rewards for evidence of "prior art," or documents that prove that someone else thought of the idea first for a disputed patent. One of the patents for which it offered a reward was the 1-Click patent. It's part of the enigma that is Jeff Bezos: Preach restraint, but if you can get away with something that improves customer service and the company's competitive edge, do it regardless of who complains. (To be sure, BountyQuest also noted that its service could also be used to *validate* patents when no prior art was discovered.) BountyQuest paid out money to three prior art submissions in an attempt to invalidate the 1-Click patent, but none of them proved strong enough to challenge the Amazon patent. BountyQuest later closed down without any significant successes.

The strongest challenge, raised several years after Bounty-Quest folded, came from a New Zealand actor named Peter Calveley (who was one of the actors hired to act out motions that were filmed and used to create computer-animated creatures for *The Lord of the Rings* movies). Calveley decided, just on a lark, to look for prior art to challenge the 1-Click patent. He found it, from a defunct online e-commerce company called Digicash. Armed with that information, the patent office ordered a reexamination of the 1-Click patent in May 2006.

That attempt failed as well. Finally, in March 2010, the patent office upheld the 1-Click patent for good—or, at least, until the patent expires—a stroke of exceptional luck for Bezos. The patent office will often rescind a patent if it seems that the patent is obvious or too broad. This time it didn't. Perhaps it depends on which individual in the patent office is doing the review. Some people feel that getting the patent upheld was like winning a crap shoot.

Bezos is still trying to enhance his luck with newer and wilder ideas. One-Click, it seems, is a step, not an end point. In June 2008, Amazon.com filed for a new patent with a Microsoft Kinect–like feature for making purchases with body movements. Anticipating computers and other devices that can track a user's movements, the new Amazon patent is titled "Movement recognition as input mechanism." Forget keypads and mice, you may soon be able to make a purchase simply by nodding your head at your computer, Kindle, or cell phone. Industry wags have dubbed it the "1-Nod patent."

It doesn't stop there, of course. You may be able to indicate such requests as how many copies of an item to order by holding up fingers, or create a password from specific motions. The patent application gives an example: "The user could set a password to three nods up and down, followed by a smile and two eyebrow raises."

This patent lists Bezos himself as the sole inventor. This illustrates two of the most important principles of an entrepreneur. Always put the customer first, even if it appears to require a decision that would decrease revenues. It's a winning strategy in the long run. And in order to get an advantage from those decisions, think of the future, not the present. Even if that future still seems to be years off. Just thinking of the idea may bring about that future more quickly. Your competitors may hate you for it, but customers will be impressed—or at least get a good laugh.

Innovations and new patents at Amazon will never cease. In December 2010, word leaked out about a new patent, for a system that enables people who get gifts through Amazon to return them even before they arrive in the mail. If Aunt Mildred has a habit of sending unwanted gifts, the patent says, the site will include an option to "convert all gifts from Aunt Mildred." (Yes, the patent includes the name of the presumably fictitious relative.) It allows the receiver to track when the well-meaning relative buys a gift for him and change it to something more desirable before it ships. Gift recipients can also apply other rules selected from the "Gift Conversion Rules Wizard," such as, "No clothes with wool," or "Convert any gift from Aunt Mildred to a gift certificate, but only after checking with me." The patent lists Bezos as the inventor.

Of course, those who dictate what constitutes proper etiquette believe such a system is in appallingly bad taste. "This idea totally misses the spirit of gift giving," sniffs Anna Post, the great-great-granddaughter of etiquette maven Emily Post and spokeswoman for the Emily Post Institute. Bezos thinks it will improve gift-giving, whether or not the giver is offended. "In some cases, concern that the gift recipient may not like a particular gift may cause the person sending the gift to be more cautious in gift selection," the patent notes.

But the idea is not only something that could please the fussy recipient, it can save Amazon millions of dollars. When a gift is returned, Amazon warehouse workers have to unpack and reshelve the old gifts and wrap, pack, and ship the new ones. And it does fit in with Bezos's desire to stay ahead with unusual innovation, a desire that has generally served the company very well.

Of course, a keen intellect, a drive to succeed, and an innate stubbornness to the point of absurdity helps. These are all signs of a born entrepreneur.

Chapter 2

Portrait of the Entrepreneur as a Young Man

Work hard, have fun, make history.

—Amazon company slogan

Jeffrey Preston Bezos was four years old when he first arrived at his grandfather's cattle ranch in Cotulla, Texas. The Lazy G is a sprawling twenty-five-thousand-acre spread in the southwest part of the state; an unspoiled habitat of mesquite and oak trees, the home of whitetail deer (popular among local hunters), wild turkeys, doves, quail, feral hogs, and sheep.

Jeff's family's Texas roots date back to the nineteenth century, when his ancestor Colonel Robert Hall left his home in Tennessee for San Antonio. Colonel Hall was an imposing man, six feet four inches tall, and in his later years had taken to wearing a colorful outfit stitched together from dozens of different types of animal pelts. "When he walked down the streets of San Antonio, the crowds would part," said Jackie Bezos, Jeff's mother. It was her great-grandfather, Bernard Vesper, who acquired the Lazy G.

Jeff's maternal grandfather, Lawrence Preston Gise, was imposing in his own way, a just-retired rocket scientist who was ready to trade in his missile research for the simple and demanding life at the ranch. (He's married to Mattie Louise Strait, who is related to country singer George Strait.) He then wanted to share that life with his grandson. From that time on, Jeff spent every summer at the ranch until he was sixteen years old. The Lazy G became a second home to the boy.

Over the years, Jeff learned to clean stalls, to brand and castrate cattle, to install plumbing, and to handle other ranch-hand tasks. One day, his grandfather towed in a dilapidated D6 Caterpillar bulldozer with a stripped transmission. Fixing it would be tough: He would have to remove a five-hundred-pound gear from the engine. No problem; he simply built himself a small crane. Jeff helped. To Bezos, fixing tractors and castrating cattle was "what I considered to be an idyllic childhood."

Years later, after becoming a hugely successful entrepreneur, Bezos said that his experience on the ranch helped sow the seeds of his entrepreneurial drive.

"One of the things that you learn in a rural area like that is self-reliance," he said. "People do everything themselves. That kind of self-reliance is something you can learn, and my grandfather was a huge role model for me: If something is broken, let's fix it. To get something new done you have to be stubborn and focused, to the point that others might find unreasonable."

His mother echoed that sentiment. "You become really self-sufficient when you work with the land," she said. "One of the things [Jeff] learned is that there really aren't any problems without solutions. Obstacles are only obstacles if you think they're obstacles. Otherwise, they're opportunities."

There's little doubt that genetics also played a role in his success. Bezos idolized his grandfather, his first mentor and role model. Preston Gise—"Pops" to Jeff—had worked on space technology and missile defense systems at the Defense Advanced Research Projects Agency, a research unit of the U.S. Defense Department. DARPA also happens to be the organization that created ARPAnet, the mysterious computer network that was later to evolve into the ubiquitous Internet. In 1964, the year Jeff was born, Pops Gise became manager of the Atomic Energy Commission's western region, supervising twenty-six thousand employees at the Sandia, Los Alamos, and Lawrence Livermore laboratories. When he retired, he traded his demanding work designing missiles and nuclear technology for the even more demanding life of a gentleman rancher.

Virtually nothing is known about Bezos's biological father, even by Jeff himself. Jeff was born Jeffrey Preston Jorgensen on January 12, 1964, in Albuquerque, New Mexico. His mother, Jacklyn (Jackie) Gise Jorgensen, an attractive, square-jawed brunette, was a seventeen-year-old recent bride working at a local bank. But his teenage father divorced his mother and left the family when Jeff was about was eighteen months old. His absent biological father faded into a nonentity in Jeff's life. "I've never been curious about him," Bezos has said. "The only time it comes up is in the doctor's office when I'm asked for my medical history. I put down that I just don't know. My real father is the guy who raised me."

Fortunately, his mother was much more successful in love the second time around. She might thank Fidel Castro for that. When Castro came to power in 1959, his regime frightened many Cuban parents into sending their children to the United States. Miguel (Mike) Bezos (the last name being a variation of "*besos*," the Spanish word for "kisses") was one of those children. In 1962, at age fifteen, he was flown to Miami by the Catholic Welfare Bureau as part of a rescue mission called Operation Peter Pan. He arrived with nothing but the clothes he was wearing and an extra shirt and pair of pants, and was shuffled off to a Catholic mission in Delaware with fifteen other young refugees.

If life was difficult in an orphanage, alone and far from home, Mike Bezos didn't show it. He thrived in his new country. He mastered English quickly, graduated from high school, and headed to New Mexico to study engineering at the University of Albuquerque. He also took a job at a local bank, where he met Jackie, who was, at that time, still pregnant with Jeff. Mike married Jackie when Jeff was about four years old. Mike adopted Jeff, giving him his name and becoming his true father. Jeff's sister, Christina, was born in 1969, and his brother, Mark, a year later. Jeff didn't learn that he and his siblings had different fathers until he was ten years old.

Mike Bezos also showed strong drive and determination. He got his degree and became a petroleum engineer at Exxon. The family followed where several job promotions took him: Houston; Pensacola, Florida; Miami. Despite repeated moves, they were a very close extended family.

Pops Gise's stubbornness was inherited by Jeff. When Jeff was three years old, his mother still had him sleeping in a crib. At that age, he could no longer abide that. "I want a real bed," he announced to his mother. As a young mother concerned about her child's safety, she said no. They argued, but she refused to give in—until the day she walked into his bedroom to find him dismantling his crib with a screwdriver, and decided he was old enough for a real bed after all.

Jeff was born with a mind capable of tenacious focus. At the Montessori elementary school he attended, he would get so absorbed in whatever task lay before him that his teachers had to pick up his chair with him in it to move him to a different task at a different table. The doggedness of a future entrepreneur was bred into his brain.

His mother and grandfather indulged his early interest in technology and tinkering with electronic gadgets and kits. "I think single-handedly we kept many Radio Shacks in business," she would later recall. Jeff spent hours in his garage rebuilding Heathkit radios, tinkering with robots, and building experimental devices. He wrapped an umbrella spine in aluminum foil for a solar cooking experiment, and even tried to build a hovercraft from an ancient Hoover vacuum. A kid who valued his privacy, he rigged up an electric alarm to warn him if his younger siblings were trying to enter his room.

Perhaps because he was influenced by his time at the Lazy G, his first career aspiration, at about age six, was to be an archaeologist. He's been known to say, "I would like to point out this was before *Indiana Jones*."

The family moved to Houston about the time Jeff started kindergarten. A few years later his parents enrolled him in the Vanguard program, a magnet program for gifted children, at River Oaks Elementary School. Attending this school for bright kids required a twenty-mile commute each way. The school now boasts about the fact that Jeff Bezos is an alumnus (along with journalist Linda Ellerbee and John Gray, the author of *Men Are from Mars, Women Are from Venus*).

And yes, he was a bookworm. Or perhaps he was showing his hypercompetitive personality at a very young age when, in the fourth grade, he got excited by a contest at school to see who could read the most Newbery Award–winning books in a year. He plowed through thirty of them (one of his favorites was *A Wrinkle in Time* by Madeleine L'Engle) but still didn't win. Kids in that school read a lot of books.

The school also gave him his first taste of computing. A company in Houston supplied his school with a computer terminal (there were no personal computers in those days) and loaned the school excess time in the company's mainframe. The terminal was connected to the mainframe by an acoustic phone modem with a cradle that held the phone handset in order to establish the connection. The setup came with a stack of manuals, but no one at the school knew how to use it. Jeff and a couple other students stayed after class to go through the manuals and figure out how to program it, but that novelty only lasted about a week. Then they discovered that the mainframe contained a primitive *Star Trek* game. From then on, all they used the computer for was playing *Star Trek*, each taking on a role of one of the characters of the TV program. Like all his other nerdy friends, he considered the choice role in the game to be that of Mr. Spock. Captain Kirk was the backup choice. If Jeff couldn't get either of those roles, he preferred to take on the persona of the starship's computer.

One day, a local writer named Julie Ray visited the school to observe the classroom. She was writing a locally published book titled *Turning on Bright Minds: A Parent Looks at Gifted Education in Texas* (which, for some unknown reason, is not on Amazon.com). Twelve-year-old Jeff was chosen as one of the clever children she decided to follow through a typical school day. She referred to him using the pseudonym Tim.

One of the stories that impressed her was his fascination with a device called the Infinity Cube, one of those things that schools for gifted children buy to turn on bright minds. The cube was lined with mirrors positioned in constantly shifting angles by small motors, so that an object placed in the cube could be re-reflected in myriad images and patterns, creating the illusion of looking into infinity. Jeff loved looking into the cube and wanted one of his own. But, he explained, since his mother thought $20 was too expensive for the toy, he decided to build one himself. He bought his own mirrors and rigged up motors to reproduce the Infinity Cube. As he explained to Ray, "The way the world is, you know, someone could tell you to press the button." But, he added, "You have to be able to think . . . for yourself."

In the book she described "Tim" as "friendly but serious" and marked by "general intellectual excellence." But she also noted that his teachers described him as "not particularly gifted in leadership."

Perhaps that was because he was a self-sufficient nerd who tended to amuse himself. Like many nerds of the twentieth century, he preferred to sit in his room or his local library, his mind buried in the fantasy world of science fiction. He read all the classics, from Robert Heinlein to Isaac Asimov to Frank Herbert and Ray Bradbury. In Cotulla, most of the books in the "tiny little Andrew Carnegie–style library" were donated by local residents, and one of them was a huge science fiction fan who donated his entire collection.

Jeff was also fond of reading about Thomas Edison and Walt Disney, two of his entrepreneurial heroes. In an interview with the Academy of Achievement, a nonprofit organization dedicated to connecting students with "the greatest thinkers and achievers of the age," he recalled, "I have always been interested in inventors and invention." He admired Edison as "the incredible inventor" and Disney as "a real pioneer and inventor," with "such big visions that no single individual could ever pull them off, unlike a lot of things that Edison worked on. Walt Disney really was able to get a big team of people working in a concerted direction." His biggest problem was that he once lost his library privileges for laughing too loud, "which was really inconvenient for me." He never minded being grounded for getting in trouble because his mother would send him to his room, where he would happily read.

In order to get him to socialize more with other kids, his parents enrolled him in a youth league team in the highly competitive Texas sport of football. Short and slightly built, he barely made the weight limit, and his mother worried that he would "get creamed." But whatever he lacked in natural leadership ability he made up for in intelligence. Within two weeks he had managed to memorize all the plays, including the roles of all eleven kids in his squad, and the coach put that skill to use by naming him defensive captain.

When he was thirteen, the family moved to Pensacola, Florida, and to Miami eighteen months later. As soon as he entered Miami Palmetto Senior High School in the Miami suburb of Pinecrest, one of Florida's top schools, he told classmates he intended to be valedictorian. Intimidated by his intellect, competitive nature, and self-confidence, they believed him. "He was always a formidable presence," recalled high school friend Joshua Weinstein.

His first summer job during high school wasn't exactly a world-changing occupation. He was a fry cook at McDonald's. But even while flipping burgers and lifting fries in and out of the vat of boiling oil, he made it a point to study the improvements in automation made by the burger chain. He was later to note, "Now the french fries raise themselves out of the oil, which, let me tell you, is a major technological innovation!"

Pinecrest was also where he met Ursula "Uschi" Werner, in his junior year. The summer after he finished high school, he and Uschi decided it was time to be their own bosses. They dreamed up their own business, the DREAM Institute (an awkward acronym for Directed REAsoning Methods), a two-week-long summer learning camp for fifth-graders. For $150 per student, they taught about fossil fuels and fission, interstellar travel and the prospect of space colonies, black holes and electric currents, and the more mysterious areas of television and advertising. In their own advertising flyer for parents printed on Jeff's dot-matrix printer, the budding entrepreneurs explained, "Our program emphasizes the use of new ways of thinking in old areas."

Their venture made the newspapers. One Wednesday in July 1982, a reporter for *The Miami Herald* visited Jeff's home to observe the class. Students Christina, Mark, Howard, Merrell, and James had gathered in Jeff's "comfortable, carpeted bedroom" as they did each weekday morning at nine. That day they had readings from *Gulliver's Travels*, *Watership Down*, and three newspaper articles (one about bass dying from pollution, another on President

Reagan's foreign policy, and a third about nuclear proliferation.) Jeff then gave a short talk about his family's Apple II computer. During a discussion of *Gulliver's Travels*, one student, James, raised a question: If the Lilliputians were so tiny compared to Gulliver, wouldn't it take them several generations to decapitate him?

Jeff and Uschi seemed to do an impressive job, and the students enjoyed the class. James, who was about to enter fifth grade, said he was learning "little neat things that I really think are neat. We study about black holes in outer space. We study about stars . . . we learned that one teaspoon of a neutron star would weigh ten billion tons." He told the reporter that the DREAM Institute was better than school. "In school, you're getting a grade. Whenever you're getting a grade for something, you always feel slightly pressured." His classmate, Merrell, also liked the informality of the classes. "You can call him Jeff instead of Mr. Bezos," he said. "It's like having a big brother teach you."

Jeff and Uschi boasted that in just two weeks they could "open new pathways of thought" in their students. "We don't just teach them something," said Jeff. "We ask them to apply it." Uschi added that they decided to teach fifth-graders because "that age is pretty creative, but also intelligent enough to understand how things work." And, they assured the reporter, they refused to make the mistake of the many teachers who underestimate their students' abilities. "You have to shock them into thinking they can do more than they think they can," said Uschi.

Although Uschi was a year ahead of Jeff, they seemed made for each other. Both were valedictorians of their graduating classes. Uschi went on to win a full scholarship to Duke University and a Rhodes Scholarship. During his high school career, Jeff attended the Student Science Training Program at the University of Florida, became a National Merit Scholar, and won the Best Science Student Award three years running and Best Math Student Award twice. He won a science prize in the prestigious Silver Knight competition for south Florida high school students, sponsored by *The Miami Herald*.

His real passion was to follow his grandfather's impressively trodden path into space science. In 2003, the by-then-wealthy Bezos announced that he was funding a program called Blue Origin, which is designing a spacecraft to give tourists a ride to the fringes of the atmosphere. He told *Wired* magazine, "The only reason I'm interested in space is because NASA inspired me when I was five years old."

In high school he also won a NASA competition by writing a paper titled "The Effect of Zero Gravity on the Aging Rate of the Common Housefly." (There's no word on how he *got* the fly into zero gravity.) For that he was shuttled to NASA's Marshall Space Flight Center in Huntsville, Alabama, for a visit. What *Star Trek* fan could ask for more?

Jeff was, in fact, obsessed with the prospect of space travel. Science fiction wasn't just a form of entertainment; to him it elevated his thoughts to the future. In his valedictorian speech, he stood up and called for the colonization of space, believing it to be humanity's destiny. He wanted to "preserve the earth" and turn it into a national park once its human inhabitants had left. After archaeology, he has said his second career choice was to be an astronaut.

Still, asked by *Time* magazine in 2001 when he first got interested in computers, he responded, "That was a love affair that really did start in the fourth grade." Rudolf Werner, the father of

Jeff's high school sweetheart, Uschi, later recalled that Jeff's fascination with space was part of a larger goal. "He said the future of mankind is not on this planet, because we might be struck by something, and we better have a spaceship out there," she said. Uschi even joked that Jeff simply wanted to become a billionaire so he could afford to build his own space station. When a reporter for *Wired* magazine asked him about these lofty goals, Bezos first laughed. But he sobered to answer the question: "I wouldn't mind helping in some way," he said. "I do think we have all our eggs in one basket."

Like most high school romances, the relationship between Jeff and Uschi didn't survive their college years. She returned to Duke, and he headed for Princeton to continue a formidable academic career.

The apocryphal story is that Jeff discovered at Princeton that he wasn't always the best at everything, leading him to switch from a major in physics to computer science. The way Jeff told the story to *Wired* magazine many years later, quantum mechanics ended his physics career. Suddenly he discovered he was no longer at the top of the class in every subject. "One of the great things Princeton taught me is that I'm not smart enough to be a physicist," he said in a rare moment of humility. (He did, however, join a Princeton group called Students for the Exploration and Development of Space.)

But he must have changed his mind sometime between graduating from high school and starting college, because in June 1982, just after he graduated from high school, *The Miami Herald* published an article about Florida valedictorians. In that article, Jeff's stated goal, according to the paper, was to study electrical engineering and business administration at Princeton—which was almost precisely what he did. His degree was in computer science and electrical engineering.

He had a special affinity for computers. Jeff the nerd loved programming. At Princeton, he has said, "I was taking all the computer classes, and actually not just learning how to hack, but learning about algorithms and some of the mathematics behind computer science, and it's fascinating. It's really a very involving and fun subject."

He has reemphasized his love of computing in other interviews. "I always had a facility with computers. I always got along well with them and they're such extraordinary tools. You can teach them to do things and then they actually do them. It's kind of an incredible tool that we've built here in the 20th Century."

In this field, he ended up with enough A-pluses at Princeton to earn a 4.2 GPA and membership in Phi Beta Kappa. For his thesis, he designed a computer system to calculate DNA sequences—a method geneticists use to find variations in sequences of genetic code, but also used to find variations in other software programs and data, including financial information.

During summer vacations from Princeton he immediately began showing off his programming skills. In the summer of 1984, his father's job at Exxon had taken the family temporarily to Norway. So Jeff joined them and took a summer job at Exxon as a programmer, developing a computer model on an IBM 4341 mainframe computer to calculate oil royalties for the firm. The following summer he traveled to Silicon Valley for a job at IBM's

Santa Teresa Research Center in San Jose. In his résumé, he boasted that he rewrote an IBM computer interface, a project for which he was allocated four weeks, but which he completed in three days.

Few people remember much about him in his Princeton years despite several extracurricular activities. He joined the Quadrangle Club, an eating club headed by David Risher, who later became a marketing executive at Amazon. But all Risher remembers about Jeff Bezos the college student was that he liked to play beer pong, a drinking game that involves batting ping-pong balls into cups of beer.

Jeff wasn't much of a ladies' man. Perhaps Princeton women aren't into beer pong. He explained his own romantic shortcomings this way: "I'm not the kind of person where women say, 'Oh, look how great he is,' a half hour after meeting me. I'm kind of goofy, and I'm not . . . it's not the kind of thing where people are going to say about me, 'Oh my God, this is what I've been looking for!'"

Another classmate, E. J. Chichilnisky, would bump into him occasionally, but today can recall nothing more than that he was "bright and motivated and organized." Still, Bezos made enough of an impression to later inspire Chichilnisky to recommend Bezos to his mother, Graciela Chichilnisky, when she started looking for smart computer scientists to join her fledgling network communications company, Fitel. That was to be the start of a meteoric career for the young computer scientist.

Chapter 3

Jeff Gets a Job

Next to Jeff Bezos's picture in the 1987 Princeton year-book is a rather bold and enigmatic quote from science fiction writer Ray Bradbury: "The Universe says No to us," it reads. "We in answer fire a broadside of flesh at it and cry Yes!"

Bezos found it to be an inspiring credo for his life. He refused to take no as an answer to anything, especially when it came to finding a job. But he was quite willing to say no to the corporations that asked him to join them. Semiconductor powerhouse Intel Corporation wooed him, as did Bell Labs, the highly regarded research arm of AT&T. Even the corporate consulting firm Anderson Consulting put in a bid.

He has said he considered becoming an entrepreneur right out of Princeton. But, he said, he "ultimately decided that it would be smarter to wait and learn a little bit more about business and the way the world works."

If he felt he wasn't quite ready to become an entrepreneur yet—for one thing, he didn't know what kind of company he wanted to start—he would at least set off on a path that would lead to

---

his own company. And that meant joining up with another entrepreneurial company. He decided to take a leap of faith with Fitel
because it was young, risky, and challenging. So he packed up and
moved to Manhattan.

Fitel's founders, Graciela Chichilnisky and Geoffrey Heal, were
professors in the economics department at Columbia University.
The company, says Professor Chichilnisky, was trying to build
"something like a mini-Internet before the Internet became popular." In fact, this was nearly a decade before the Internet took off
and changed everybody's lives (including Bezos's). The system
Fitel was building, called Equinet, linked different computers at
brokerage firms, investment firms, and banks over a network to
allow them to conduct stock trades among themselves.

Fitel was focused on Wall Street investors, the first in a string
of such companies that Jeff would join. Contrary to popular belief,
however, he was not himself an investment banker. It was a time
when investment banks were trying to harness computer power
to increase the efficiency of their trades, a trend that continues
even today. It was Jeff's knack for wrangling computer code that
the companies were after.

Fitel had hired fifteen extremely smart young computer scientists, including Jeff, who was employee number eleven. Jeff worked
on the communications protocols, a key—and complicated—part
of the system that enabled different, incompatible computer networks to understand and exchange data with each other. "The
communications protocols were the most challenging," says Chichilnisky. She designed the system and Jeff built it. "It was damn
well engineered because Jeff did it himself," she says. "He was

one of the best communications engineers I had. It didn't seize, it didn't hang up. It worked. Period."

If the universe didn't say no to the system, most people in the industry did. They didn't believe it could be done. The system was first installed at Salomon Brothers, sending thousands of trades back and forth through the network to varied computers at different banks. It was so impressive and worked so well, says Chichilnisky, that the traders had trouble accepting that it was real. "Salomon thought it was a trick," she recalls. "They couldn't believe it was happening."

In less than a year, Jeff was promoted from a manager-level position (of administration and development) to an associate director position (of technology and business development). That essentially made him second-in-command at the firm. At twenty-three years old, Jeff was managing a dozen programmers in Fitel's different offices.

Nevertheless, he was a restless soul, still hoping to expand his horizons and learn the secrets of becoming an entrepreneur. A year after Bezos joined her firm, Chichilnisky left to raise her young child. One year after she left, Bezos followed suit. It was April 1988, just two years after he'd joined Fitel.

He joined Bankers Trust, another company "working at the intersection of computers and finance," as he put it. He started out as an assistant vice president and became Bankers Trust's youngest vice president at twenty-six, ten months after joining the firm, running yet another engineering department that created a communications network, this one called BTWorld. This software program was installed on PCs on desktops at a hundred large corporations, allowing them to communicate with Bankers Trust's computers. That allowed BT's clients to remotely track the performance of the pension funds and profit-sharing plans that BT invested and managed for them. It replaced the periodic paper reports that the bank used to mail to its clients. Instead, the bank was able to deliver up-to-the-minute performance results electronically.

Once again, this was something that people in the status quo thought couldn't be done, especially on the primitive PCs of the time, which most people considered to be little better than toys. Many people at the bank thought that "this was something that couldn't be done, that shouldn't be done, and that the traditional way of delivering the reports in hard copy was better," recalled Harvey Hirsch, a former vice president at Bankers Trust and Jeff's boss at the time. Some of them were "vehemently opposed to what he was proposing," said Hirsch.

But Jeff wore down the resistance. "He sees different ways of doing things and better ways of doing things," said Hirsch. "He told the naysayers, 'I believe in this new technology and I'm going to show you how it's going to work'—and he did. At the end of the day he proved them all wrong. He has no trouble puncturing someone's balloon if he thinks they're proposing to do something the wrong way or in an inappropriate way. He'll argue his point of view very persuasively. That doesn't mean that he didn't break some eggs in the process because he proved people wrong, but I don't think he ever did it in a way that angered or infuriated people. It was all very professional."

During Jeff's time at Bankers Trust, he also kept an eye out for the opportunity to become a true entrepreneur, and it almost happened. In 1989 he met a Merrill Lynch investment banking analyst named Halsey Minor, another young man with aspirations of becoming an entrepreneur. Minor had been building an internal network for Merrill that could link information, graphics, and animation together, much like today's Internet. He decided the project could be spun out as a separate business.

Merrill Lynch gave Minor money to start his own company in order to build the network. But Minor became more ambitious; he wanted to create a network that would send news stories to subscribers based on their individual interests. Jeff linked up with him on the project in 1990, and Merrill considered providing funding for the company. Bezos and Minor, twenty-six and twenty-five, respectively, seemed to be heading down the entrepreneurial path. But that venture was not meant to be. Within a few weeks, Merrill executives decided not to provide funds.

Both men did later became successful entrepreneurs anyway— Minor went on to start the CNET news service, which he later sold, becoming a millionaire. With his first entrepreneurial hopes dashed, Bezos began looking for a more challenging technical and business opportunity. He wanted to get out of financial services and into something more entrepreneurial and technologically focused, a company that could bring about a new wave of automation that would revolutionize business. He sent out his résumé to headhunters. But this time he wanted a real technology company, not another Wall Street firm.

One of the headhunters called him and said, "I know you said you would kill me if I even proposed the finance thing, but there's this opportunity that's actually a very unusual financial company."

That company was D. E. Shaw. It was founded in 1988 by David

Shaw to create a newfangled computer-automated trading system for Wall Street. Shaw was a computer science professor at Columbia University who was lured to Wall Street to help computerize stock trading systems, and then started his own company. At the time, computer software was already being used to track small differences in stock prices around the world, allowing arbitrageurs to buy the stock at one price and immediately sell it for a profit at the higher price. But the traders still had to analyze the data and make the trades. Shaw's computer systems took the humans out of the equation. As soon as the computer system found price discrepancies, it would automatically buy and sell the stocks in a fraction of the time a human could do it. That gave firms who used this system a substantial advantage in the split-second trading world of arbitrage.

David Shaw was the kind of man Jeff could relate to. He had earned a Ph.D. in computer science from Stanford. From there he became an assistant professor of computer science at Columbia University, doing research on massively parallel supercomputers, in which hundreds of computers are linked together to work as one giant computer. Morgan Stanley lured him into electronic trading by offering him six times his professor's salary and enormous financial resources. A year and a half later, he decided he could do more interesting things in computer trading on his own, and started D. E. Shaw.

His company developed a reputation as an incredible place for mathematicians and computer scientists to work, one that only hired about 1 percent of those who applied. Jeff was one who was accepted into this elite group.

The Wall Street Journal described D. E. Shaw as being "in the vanguard of computerized selling," while *Fortune* magazine called it "the most technologically sophisticated firm on [Wall] Street" and added that David Shaw's reputation was "an amalgam of Einstein, Midas, and Rasputin."

Bezos liked him. Years later, he described Shaw as "one of those people who has a completely developed left brain and a completely developed right brain. He's artistic, articulate, and analytical. It's just a pleasure to talk to someone like that." The feeling was mutual. Shaw described Bezos as "a pleasurable person to talk to" who was "also very entrepreneurial." He was the last person Jeff would ever work for.

Bezos was twenty-six years old when he was hired, in December 1990, in the position of vice president. He was promoted to senior vice president a few years later. One of four managers at Shaw, he created and led a twenty-four-person team exploring new market opportunities.

Still, Jeff was an unusual corporate executive. With a highly technical mind and methodical approach to business, he struck some of the people he worked for as a bit strange. What got him ahead was his ability to take in the big picture as well as deal with the most demanding details.

Bezos "has no limits," says former boss Chichilnisky. "It's the most amazing thing. He has no psychological barriers."

Halsey Minor would agree with Chichilnisky. Eight years after their ill-fated venture together, the Silicon Valley magazine *Red Herring* ran a feature story listing the top twenty entrepreneurs of 1997 (both Minor and Bezos made the list). In that feature, Minor was quoted praising Bezos's multiple talents. "Outside of Bill Gates, I think there are few other people who share Jeff's deep technical understanding and combine it with highly refined strategic and tactical instincts," he said. Minor also told the UK publication *The Independent*, "Jeff is one of the few hardcore developers who can do other things." He also noted that "he always had the dream of starting his own company."

Some people found Bezos to be very personable, others did not. Chichilnisky thought he was a bit cold. "I didn't think he was a very 'nice' person," says Chichilnisky. "I liked him, but he was not warm. I'm not criticizing him, not a bit. It was like he could be a Martian for all I knew. A well-meaning, nice Martian."

Being something of a Martian and dedicated to his work, he was not the most sought-after bachelor in Manhattan. So he decided to spice up his love life and become what he was later to describe as a "professional dater." He took a particularly geeky approach to the problem.

Having always been the methodical type, he set about trying to find a great girlfriend by using the same methodology that Wall Street bankers use to find a great investment: He set up a "deal flow" chart. Wall Streeters' deal flow charts are listings of all the attributes a deal must have before they will take a chance on it, in order to remain objective and not be influenced by an emotional response. Likewise, Jeff's "women flow" chart listed the criteria his potential partners had to have before he would consummate a deal. "The number one criterion was that I wanted a woman who could get me out of a Third World prison," he later said. He figured that was the best way to get the idea across. "What I really wanted was someone resourceful. But nobody knows what you mean when you say, 'I'm looking for a resourceful woman.' If I tell somebody I'm looking for a woman who can get me out of a Third

World prison, they start thinking Ross Perot—they have something they can hang their hat on!"

Most straight men would not find H. Ross Perot, a former dealmaker and onetime presidential candidate, to be the model for their ideal girlfriend's mentality. But to Jeff, it meant efficiency. "Life's too short to hang out with people who aren't resourceful," he said.

For some reason, the women flow chart didn't work. But Bezos also ended up with another perk from D. E. Shaw. Without the aid of a women flow chart, he met MacKenzie Tuttle, one of his research associates at the firm. Also a graduate of Princeton (in 1992), she was an aspiring writer and a former research assistant to novelist Toni Morrison as Morrison was working on *Jazz*. Although she has never said how she might spring Jeff from a Third World prison, he was impressed with his young researcher. MacKenzie was working on a novel of her own, titled *The Testing of Luther Albright*. It got a great review from Morrison, although it currently doesn't quite make it within the top two million best-selling books on Amazon. They were married in 1993, and Bezos's life marched on toward his real goal: finally becoming an entrepreneur.

Chapter 4

Jeff Discovers the Internet

David Shaw ended up being the one who set Bezos off on the path that led to opportunity. In 1994, he asked Bezos to look at this new thing becoming all the buzz, something called the Internet. It was a piece of technology that seemed to be coming together with elements that just might create opportunities for a company that used computer networks to conduct stock trades.

Until recently, the Internet had been mostly used as a network that allowed universities, research labs, and government institutions to exchange information. One key step toward change was taken in 1990, when Tim Berners-Lee created the first Internet browser, called World Wide Web. Another came in 1991, when the Internet was opened up to commercial use for the first time. It took several more years before these changes caught on and spread to popular awareness. In 1993, a government-funded group at the University of Illinois at Urbana-Champaign created a new generation of Web browser called Mosaic, a wonderful, graphics-based browser. The following year, a very astute Silicon Valley venture capitalist named John Doerr decided to recruit a bright young man, Marc Andreessen, from the Mosaic team in Illinois to move to Silicon Valley and start a Web browser company. That same year the company, called Netscape, launched its browser, Navigator.

Shaw decided the Internet had a future, and gave Bezos the task of finding the opportunities there. In the spring of 1994, he began researching the Internet, and was impressed with what he found. Primarily, he says, he came across an important statistic: The Internet was growing at 2,300 percent a year! "You know, things just don't grow that fast. It's highly unusual, and that started me thinking, 'What kind of business plan might make sense in the context of that growth?'"

Those numbers sound incredibly impressive, although that growth was starting from a very small base. An annual growth rate of 2,300 percent annually simply means the population grows by a factor of 23 every year. How impressive that is depends on the starting point. A club of 100 people that grows by 2,300 percent annually, for example, ends up with 2,400 members after a year. But those numbers quickly get crazy—assuming that growth rate continues. After the third year of growth the club would boast 1.4 million members.

Similarly, from a very small base, a bacterial infection can quickly turn into billions of infectious organisms, an arithmetic phenomenon of which Bezos was fully aware. "I had never seen anything grow so fast, and I don't think many people had, except for perhaps in a petri dish," he said in a speech to the Commonwealth Club in Silicon Valley.

That's great for bacteria. Such growth rates, however, are *not*

sustainable outside of a petri dish. International Data Corporation has numbers going back to December 1995, when it estimates
that sixteen million people were using the Internet. IDC puts the
Internet population at thirty-six million at the end of 1996, for a
growth rate of just 125 percent. Growth was just under 100 percent
for the next two years.

Still, that doesn't take away from Jeff's ability to recognize a
good thing growing when he saw it. The short version of the story
is simply that Jeff knew there would be a huge Internet population
in short order. (IDC says there are more than 1.7 billion people
online these days, which is approaching one-quarter of the world's
population.) Fast growth means opportunity, in most people's
dreams. Twitter accounts, for example, grew by 1,500 percent in
2009, although it has not figured out how to make a profit off that
growth. Jeff's job, and his genius, was to find a way to make a fortune off this phenomenon.

Shaw recognized it as well. By 1996, D. E. Shaw was spinning off
Internet companies, including the free, ad-supported email service called Juno, and Farsight, an online service with aspirations of
managing everybody's finances through Shaw's Web site, including banking, brokerage, and insurance services. But the most out-
standing spinoff from D. E. Shaw was the one Jeff kept for himself.

Most successful entrepreneurs start a company because they're
passionate about the business they want to enter—Bill Gates creating software with the goal of putting a computer on everyone's
desk, Steve Jobs pioneering a new personal computer with a design
that would set gold standards, or Larry Page and Sergey Brin creating a search engine that could bring all the world's information to

everyone. But Bezos was simply interested in the fact that growth of the Internet meant *somebody* was going to make a fortune or two from the phenomenon, and he wanted one for himself.

He didn't set out to build the world's biggest bookstore simply because he loved books, although he does love them, as shown by his voracious appetite for books in his youth. He wanted to simply create a hit company by leveraging his business and technology skills. It didn't matter what the business was, as long as it had huge potential. He realized the Internet would become an enormous gathering place, and where people gathered, there was an opportunity to sell them something, if one understood the unique characteristics of that new environment and figured out how to exploit it properly. He began to dream of becoming the world's largest Internet retailer—perhaps the world's largest retailer, period.

But he also realized that the best approach was to start by focusing on one market, to figure out the needs of that market and match them to the needs and capabilities of the Internet. Once he was established in one market, he would be able to figure out other markets as well. His big challenge was to figure out what product to sell. To answer that question, he created a deal flow chart to analyze several opportunities. He made a list of twenty possible products. Which one offered the best set of features for quickly building an Internet presence? "I was looking for something that you could only do online, something that couldn't be replicated in the physical world," he said. The answer turned out to be books.

Imagine the criteria an ambitious young executive with a penchant for computers would put on a deal flow list.

Familiar product: Everyone knows what a book is. When ordering a particular title online, nobody has to worry about whether it is a cheap knockoff or an imitation, as they might with, say, consumer electronics.

Large market size: Computer software and music might be reasonable bets. In 1994, according to U.S. Census Bureau data, nearly $7 billion worth of PC software applications were sold in North American retail stores in 1994. That same year, however, $19 billion worth of books were sold in the United States. Further, almost $2 billion of the software applications sold that year were produced by just one publisher: Microsoft. Entering the software business would make Jeff heavily dependent on just one producer, making it difficult to negotiate price reductions.

As for music, there were 300,000 CD titles for sale, compared to 3 million different books available around the world. "Books are incredibly unusual in one respect, and that is that there are more items in the book category than there are in any other category by far," he was later to recall. In 1994, 513 million copies of books were sold, and 17 best sellers sold over one million copies. And on average, American consumers spent $79 per person on books in 1994, compared to $56 per person on recorded music.

Competition: There were two large bookstore chains, Barnes & Noble and Borders Group, with a combined market share of 25 percent. An uncountable number of independent bookstores accounted for another 21 percent of sales. The remainder were not sold through bookstores at all, but through other outlets such as supermarkets, general-purpose retailers, book clubs, and mail-order catalogs.

Most bookstores also carried a very limited inventory. Although they could easily order a book if a customer wanted it, that's just not as satisfying in an instant-gratification world. Barnes & Noble and Borders were converting large structures, such as bowling alleys and movie theaters, into 60,000-square-foot superstores, but even these carried no more than 175,000 titles.

The growing popularity of mail-order books also provided a basis on which to build a virtual bookstore. As for direct competition, there were a couple of online offerings already, but they were primitive approaches. In 1991, a handful of specialty book publishers and retailers, such as Computer Literacy Bookstore (clbooks .com), O'Reilly & Associates (ora.com), and the Stanford University Bookstore, allowed the few people with online accounts (using online Bulletin Boards, or pre-Web Internet communications systems) to order books through email. In 1992, a start-up called, naturally, Books.com, launched a similar service, and the following year posted an online database of 40,000 titles. There was clearly room for a more sophisticated system of online book selling.

Acquiring inventory: Most importantly, there was a ready source of wholesale books. Two distributors, Ingram Book Group and Baker & Taylor, dominated the market. Their warehouses contained about 400,000 titles. Small, independent bookstores relied on these distributors, rather than the publishers, to supply them with titles, and Jeff could tap into this ready source. The distributors both had warehouses located strategically around the U.S. and could deliver books within a couple of days. When customers requested books that a store did not stock, most bookstores ordered the books from one of those two distributors.

Creating a database of books for sale: Finally, the wholesalers had already set the stage for the digital age. Bezos attended a meeting of the American Booksellers Association (ABA) and discovered that all books for sale were given an ISBN number. The ISBN (International Standard Book Number) was created in the

1960s, then standardized by the International Organization for Standardization (ISO) in 1970. That made it easier to create a database of books and search for them by their ISBN numbers. In the late 1980s, Ingram and Baker & Taylor had upgraded their inventory list from microfiche, which an individual had to scan through manually, to a digital format that clerks could search through on a computer. It seemed to Bezos as if all the information about books "had been meticulously organized so it could be put online."

Discount opportunities: In the early 1990s, Crown Books had opened up hundreds of discount stores, forcing the major booksellers to follow suit for the first time. But the cost of real estate for the stores and the cost of maintaining inventories meant their ability to discount books and still make a profit was limited. An online store that could order books directly from the distributors instead of keeping its own inventory would have a huge price advantage.

Shipping costs: Like software and music CDs, books are easy to ship through the mail at book rates or with overnight delivery services. At eight ounces to a couple pounds, a book is heavier than a CD or software (depending on the size of the manual) but lighter than computers or many other consumer electronics products.

Online potential: Finally, software programs could sort, search, and organize book titles and categories, making them easier to find and buy online. The largest bookstores carried just 175,000 titles, but Bezos knew that software could sort through a million titles in a database, as long as he had a couple of reasonably powerful computers.

Jeff was amazed by what he found when he analyzed the potential of selling different products online. Books appeared to be by far the most eligible partner for a dance with e-commerce. To

most people, the idea would seem too simple to start a revolution. In reality, what Jeff created was simply a mail-order book
service that used the Internet to place orders. But he knew it could
be a very *big* system for placing orders. "I didn't think of it," John
Ingram, chairman of Ingram Book Company, was later to confess.
"Before 1995, I'm not sure I knew what the Internet was."

Jeff told David Shaw that he had found the right opportunity.
But selling books was a big leap for a financial services firm, and
Shaw apparently rejected the idea.

Jeff thought about it, and decided this was an opportunity he
couldn't pass by. He told Shaw he was going to start a company on
his own, and Shaw took him on a long walk to try to talk him out
of it. Why leave a stable, high-paying job with substantial bonuses
for the vagaries and uncertainty of a start-up? Of course, Shaw
had done the same thing when he started his company, but Jeff
considered this argument deeply.

Once again, the nerdy, list-making aspect of his personality helped him decide. In a speech at Lake Forest College in 1998
(where he was given an honorary degree), Jeff recalled that he
created a "regret minimization framework." Once he was old and
looking back on his life, what would he regret the most if he made
either decision? "A lot of people live their lives this way," he con-
fessed. But, he added, "Very few are nerdy and dorky enough to
call it a 'regret minimization framework,' but that was what I came
up with."

His conclusion: "I knew that when I was eighty there was no
chance that I would regret having walked away from my 1994
Wall Street bonus in the middle of the year. I wouldn't even have
remembered that. But I did think there was a chance that I might

—

regret significantly not participating in this thing called the Internet, that I believed passionately in. I also knew that if I had tried and failed, I wouldn't regret that."

Once he made that decision, he knew it was time to go, and go quickly. "When something is growing 2,300 percent a year, you have to move fast," he said in his speech. "A sense of urgency becomes your most valuable asset." He knew that the company that got the earliest start would have the easiest time capturing the early customers and making a name for the business.

So he told Shaw he decided to start a company to sell books online, and gave notice. It was the summer of 1994.

Now that he had his idea for a new company and a way to make it work with the new technology the Internet was likely to provide, he had to start building a company. That meant finding some people to help him. Fortunately, his years in business had provided the connections he needed to find some good people. More importantly, he had the self-confidence of Muhammad Ali, the enthusiasm of John Kennedy, and the brains of Thomas Edison. He had what was needed to persuade others to join him in his bold new quest.

Chapter 5

Three Nerds and an Accountant

The Internet is like alcohol in some sense. It accentuates what you would do anyway. If you want to be a loner, you can be more alone. If you want to connect, it makes it easier to connect.

—Esther Dyson

The first step in building a company is to find good people. And that can be a problem. How does one convince people to join a venture with almost no funding, and aspirations to create the world's biggest bookstore without actually creating a physical store and without actually stocking any books? Bezos's original idea was that he could simply order a book from the distributors once he had a buyer, and turn around and ship it off to the customer as soon as it arrived at his warehouse.

The process begins by tapping your business connections. It's often a matter of moving from one person to another, and from that person to yet another. It's a process encapsulated today in online networks such as the LinkedIn social networking site, where your connections can introduce you to other connections, who can introduce you to still more connections. Bezos didn't have LinkedIn, but he had made a lot of business connections, and he was good at exploiting them by phone. Bezos was prohibited from hiring people from D. E. Shaw, but he could use his comrades there as a starting point. MacKenzie wasn't the only happy connection Bezos had from Shaw. Another was a guy named Peter Laventhol. Since Bezos was looking for engineers, Laventhol told him about a friend from grad school at Stanford, a guy named Herb, who was living in California and kicking around his own ideas for an Internet-based business with a friend. And *that* friend was Sheldon J. "Shel" Kaphan, a well-known engineer who had been bouncing from start-up to start-up in Silicon Valley in search of one that would become the next Apple Computer. It was early 1994.

Kaphan had a B.A. in mathematics from the University of California in Santa Cruz, the laid-back university and surfer town where he grew up. But by the mid-1990s, Santa Cruz, seventy miles down the coast from San Francisco and thirty-five miles southwest of San Jose, had become something of a Silicon Valley suburb. Several technology companies had moved or grown up there, and people (like Kaphan) who preferred the coastal, hippie-ish culture of Santa Cruz commuted to Silicon Valley. Kaphan's reputation as a superb programmer had spread throughout Silicon Valley over the twenty years he had worked there, but he had not yet ended up at a successful start-up where he could make his fortune.

It wasn't from a lack of trying. In 1985 he became senior scientist at Lucid, Inc., an artificial intelligence software company founded a year earlier by scientists from Lawrence Livermore National Labs, Carnegie-Mellon University, and MIT. Kaphan left in 1989, and Lucid went bankrupt in 1994. Kaphan then joined another high-profile company, one-year-old Frox, Inc., as senior software developer. Frox was developing "revolutionary" home entertainment systems, including the much-publicized Frox wand, a one-button universal remote. Frox had attracted engineers from Lucasfilm, Droidworks, Xerox PARC, Sun Microsystems, and Apple Computer. But Frox didn't have the design flair of Steve Jobs. Kaphan lasted about three years, the company lasted twenty. In 1992 Kaphan joined Kaleida Labs, a joint venture between Apple and IBM, which created a digital multimedia player for computers, and wanted to create a similar program for television set-top boxes. Founded in 1991, it was folded into Apple in 1995.

In the spring of 1994, just about the time Bezos was looking for an idea that he could turn into a good Web-based business, Herb and Shel were doing the same thing. But the pair felt that they knew what their previous start-ups had lacked. "We were primarily technical people and we knew enough to know we needed to link up with a good businessperson," recalls Kaphan. "We knew that whatever we did we would need help with fund-raising, marketing, and management, at least."

Herb and Shel started tapping their own networks to find that businessperson. They reached out to Laventhol, who passed the information on to Bezos. Jeff flew out to Santa Cruz to meet them.

The trio met for breakfast at a café in Santa Cruz to exchange ideas. They got along well. "I thought Jeff was energetic and primed to succeed, with a history of succeeding," Kaphan wrote to me in an email. "He seemed, when I met him, to be cheerful of disposition and with a good sense of humor. He was also obviously well-versed in the ways of the financial community and I thought that was key to success, as I had worked for a number of places where the management lacked a sufficient degree of skill in that area. It seemed at the beginning that he was willing to trust me to do my job and would give me the space to do it in the best way that I saw fit, which was important to me." Mainly, he says, Bezos struck him as "someone who was born and bred to be successful."

Kaphan also liked the idea of creating an online bookstore. While less ambitious than the highly advanced technology his previous start-ups were trying to commercialize, it seemed to have a better chance of succeeding. "Having worked for a large number of more technologically oriented start-ups that didn't do so well, I liked the idea of one in which I could easily describe where the revenue stream was going to come from," he recalls. "At that time both Jeff and I believed Amazon could succeed as a relatively small business, compared to what it eventually became. I liked that too."

Plus, it reminded Kaphan of an enjoyable, although brief, time he had spent in 1970 working for Stewart Brand's Whole Earth Truck Store, precursor of the *Whole Earth Catalog*. "I saw Amazon's mission as a continuation of certain aspects of that same mission: to supply hard to find tools (mainly information-based tools) to a far-flung clientele who might not have easy access to those tools in their local communities," he says.

Bezos offered to hire both Kaphan and Herb. Kaphan even started looking around for office space in Santa Cruz, hoping that Bezos might decide to put down his entrepreneurial roots there. The conversation between Bezos, Kaphan, and his friend lasted for several months as Bezos made his plans.

Bezos had not yet decided where to base his company. While

most entrepreneurs were moving to Silicon Valley as the obvious place to become an entrepreneur, Jeff took a different approach: Yes, he would create another deal flow list to help decide.

He came up with three criteria: It had to be a place with an established population of entrepreneurs and software programmers. He wanted to locate the business in a state with a relatively low population because only residents of that state would have to pay sales tax on the products he sold. He wanted a city near a warehouse run by one of the major book distributors so he could get supplies quickly. But the city also had to be a major metropolitan hub with an airport offering a lot of daily flights so he could deliver books to his customers quickly.

The city that best suited the criteria was not in Silicon Valley. Bezos found that Seattle, Washington—the birthplace of Microsoft—best fit the bill. Because of Microsoft, Seattle was becoming a major technology center, attracting other research centers from tech companies such as Nintendo and Adobe Systems, and was spinning off entrepreneurial companies, including the streaming media company RealNetworks (then called Progressive Networks), started by a former Microsoft executive. In many ways, the greater Seattle area was a younger version of Silicon Valley—and certainly a much cheaper place to live. And Ingram Book Group's largest U.S. distribution center was a short six-hour drive away in Roseburg, Oregon.

Seattle was also the home of Nicholas J. Hanauer, a friend of one of Bezos's former Shaw colleagues. Hanauer was a senior executive at his family's business, Pacific Coast Feather Company. The company provided feathers for pillows, comforters, and mattress pads. In fact, it provided a lot of feathers—enough to bring in $200 million a year in revenues. Hanauer was doing well.

One day, Hanauer decided to visit a friend in Manhattan. The friend invited Bezos along for lunch with him and Hanauer. Although they probably didn't have many mutual business interests, between bird feathers and computer networks, Jeff and Hanauer hit it off.

A couple of years later, when Hanauer heard that Bezos was going to start an e-commerce company, he called him in Manhattan. Hanauer told Bezos that he was interested in investing, that Seattle was "the center of the universe," and that Bezos should move out there to create his new company. That gave an even stronger incentive for moving to Seattle.

But from this point on, the story becomes less certain. The well-known scenario is that Bezos didn't know where they would end up even as he and MacKenzie packed up and prepared to leave Manhattan in the summer of 1994. He was apparently also contemplating sites in Nevada. Another legend about Jeff's fondness for taking bold risks recounts that, when the moving company packing up his Manhattan apartment asked for the destination, Jeff told them to just start driving west, while he and MacKenzie got in a 1988 Chevy Blazer donated by his father and did the same. (It turns out that story is a bit of an abbreviation. Jeff and MacKenzie flew to Texas to get the car, and drove from there.) The day after they left, Jeff made up his mind and called Hanauer, said he was on his way, and asked if he could store his things at Hanauer's house. Then he called the movers with their destination. Jeff and MacKenzie arrived about a week after their furniture.

Kaphan was disappointed that Bezos didn't choose California. "The change of venue from Santa Cruz made it a lot harder for me to decide to do it," he says. In fact, his friend Herb decided not to make the move. But Kaphan decided to throw his programming talents into the pool. "I was convinced to join because I believed in the mission of making a wide selection of books available to people all over the world, because I believed that I could have a significant part in making it happen, and that Jeff was someone who was likely to succeed. I also thought it was going to be fun, and I was tired of the kind of jobs that were available to me in Silicon Valley."

So Kaphan rented a U-Haul to move some of his possessions to Washington. Still, he kept his house and much of his furniture in Santa Cruz, just in case the whole thing failed. Kaphan was Amazon.com's first employee and a key partner in launching the business. Within a couple of years, he made a fortune when Amazon went public. He stayed for five years.

Bezos also had to decide what to call the company. He would need a name if he was going to incorporate a business. On his drive west, he called a Seattle attorney whom Hanauer had recommended, Todd Tarbert, to incorporate the company, and told him the name was to be "Cadabra, Inc.," a play on the magician's chant of "abracadabra." It was apparent that name was a problem when Tarbert asked, "Cadaver?" "I thought, 'Oh, boy, that's not going to work,'" Bezos recalled. When Kaphan moved from California and found out the name of the company he was joining, he said the discovery "almost caused me to return to Santa Cruz."

But Cadabra was incorporated in July 1994, just as Jeff and MacKenzie arrived in Seattle. Seven months later Jeff chose Amazon for a new name because it began with an A, would come up high in any alphabetical listings, and because, as the world's largest river, it reflected his ambitions for his company. Plus, it was easy to spell. "One of the things that people don't think about but is really important is that online, you get to places by being able to spell their name," he noted. But he insisted it always be referred to as "Amazon.com" to show that it was a new breed of business. Amazon became the first successful "dot-com" company, before the dot-com crash turned it into a derogatory term.

Jeff and MacKenzie spent five days at Hanauer's house before finding their own three-bedroom rental, at 10704 NE 28th Street in the Seattle suburb of Bellevue. It cost them $890 a month. He chose it in part because it had one crucial requirement—a garage, so that Jeff could boast of having a garage start-up like Silicon Valley legends from Hewlett-Packard on. The garage had actually been converted into a recreation room, but Jeff figured it was close enough. "We thought it was important for that garage start-up legitimacy," he said. "Unfortunately, it was an enclosed garage, so we didn't get the full legitimacy. But it did have no insulation and a huge, black, pot-bellied stove for heat right in the center of the garage." (The house was later sold, in 1998, for $182,000. In 2009, because of the growth of the technology business in Seattle and the appreciation in the cost of living in the area, it was sold for $625,000. Neither buyer knew its history as Amazon.com's birthplace, although both buyers worked at technology companies.)

Ready to start work on his start-up, Bezos needed a business plan, of course. Or did he? Another Bezos legend claims that Jeff wrote his business plan on a laptop in the passenger seat while MacKenzie drove from Manhattan to Seattle. Others at Amazon, however, have said that he still hadn't finished writing his plan a year after the company was started.

He managed to start a company without a business plan

because he didn't need to raise money yet. Ever wonder how entrepreneurs get so rich? The wealthiest—like Microsoft's Bill Gates—manage to build up some value in their company before asking venture capitalists for cash. Gates did that by creating a company that was almost immediately profitable. Amazon.com represented a new approach to entrepreneurship, one that would be used by thousands of dot-com companies in the late 1990s: He went for years without a profit, or even trying to become profitable.

Instead, Bezos used his own money. Having been well paid in his previous jobs, he had enough savings to fund the company for several months. In 1994, Bezos bought 10.2 million shares of Amazon.com stock for $10,000—or one-tenth of a penny per share. When Amazon.com went public three years later at $18 per share, this initial investment from Bezos was worth almost $184 million.

Ten grand, however, doesn't get you far. By the end of 1994 he had also given Amazon.com interest-free loans totaling $44,000. Fortunately, he had friends and family to help out as well. In February 1995 he raised just over $100,000 by selling 582,528 shares to his father, Miguel Bezos, for 17.17 cents per share, enough to keep the company running for the first six or seven months.

His family was willing to invest because they had as much faith in him as he did himself. His mother has said the family invested in Jeff, not in the concept he was pitching, since they had never heard of the Internet before. Bezos knew that only about 10 percent of start-ups succeed even modestly, but gave himself about a 30 percent chance, and told his parents up front that those were the odds. He told his family they should only make the investment if they were prepared to lose it. That kind of honesty is crucial for an entrepreneur, who might otherwise be too intimidated by the odds of failure to make the risky moves necessary to win. "That's actually a very liberating expectation, expecting to fail," he has said. Of course, his family made out very well in the end. That hundred grand worth of stock would be worth over $10 million in a couple of years.

When Jeff got to Seattle, he looked around for other smart software jockeys recommended to him by friends and colleagues. He tapped the University of Washington Computer Science & Engineering Department, which had a great reputation in computing.

Brian Bershad, who headed UW's Science & Engineering Department, was skeptical of the venture when Bezos told him about it. But he circulated an email to people affiliated with his department, and one person decided to take a chance: Paul Barton-Davis. (He reverted to his original name of Paul Davis after his divorce from his wife in 2001, but is now so famous on the Internet by the previous name that it still sticks to him.) Davis was a molecular biologist from London who immigrated to Seattle in 1989 and became a software engineer. At a Seattle company called ScenicSoft, Inc., he designed programs for the open-source UNIX software system, the operating system Amazon.com would also use. In the fall of 1993 he joined the UW Computer Science & Engineering Department, and he became the Web master for the first open Web network (one not restricted to an individual or small group of companies) in the Pacific Northwest.

Davis had aspirations to work with a start-up, however, and didn't last long at the university. The following summer he became a programmer for the Seattle Internet company called USPAN. He created a hyperlink program (which allows Internet surfers to jump from one Internet site to another by clicking on the link) but abandoned it when he discovered the Mosaic Web browser. Mosaic was developed at the National Center for Supercomputing Applications (NCSA) at the Urbana-Champaign campus of the University of Illinois, becoming the first (and, many people still feel, the best) browser to take advantage of the newly created World Wide Web. Davis hoped to integrate his hyperlink program into that browser, and contacted Marc Andreessen, a smart computer science student at the University of Illinois who codeveloped Mosaic. If that collaboration had worked, Davis might have joined Netscape Communications, which Andreessen later founded, and made his fortune there. But Mosaic and Davis's hyperlink system were too incompatible, and Davis had to look elsewhere to join the new wave of bright engineers and entrepreneurs hoping to build new products and companies on the Internet.

So Davis decided to check out this new company starting up in Seattle. He was initially reluctant to join such a raw company, but he was impressed with Jeff and his vision of creating a virtual bookstore online. "I thought he would be interesting to work for," said Davis. He met with Kaphan in October and the two seemed compatible, so he joined the team as employee number two (the first of many former UW engineers Bezos would hire).

Neither Kaphan nor Davis had much experience creating the kind of retailing or business software that Amazon.com needed, but Jeff's philosophy was to hire people with the most talent rather than the most experience. After all, they were trying to do something new, and experience with legacy software could be more of a hindrance than a help. It's a philosophy promoted by Silicon Valley start-ups that the best people are those who don't know that something "can't be done," and therefore will figure out how er6

to do it. Bezos is a strong believer in this philosophy. He and these two men developed the core software that launched Amazon.com, programs that ran the company for years.

The third employee of the company was Jeff's wife, MacKenzie. She handled the phone calls, ordering and purchasing, secretarial duties, and accounting. She had to learn the last job by taking up a simple accounting program, Peachtree PC Accounting Software. Jeff didn't hire a real accountant until the summer of 1996.

At the time, Amazon.com was still a bare-bones garage start-up, with nothing but a desk made from a door and a network router Jeff had bought online from the Internet Shopping Service, no doubt in order to check out an online shopping network. He also checked out the capabilities of the other fledgling online booksellers. He bought *How to Be a Computer Consultant* from Computer Literacy's clbooks.com.

It was just a few months after arriving in Seattle that Bezos decided to take a class on how to create a bookstore. Howorth, the instructor who gave the famous lecture on customer service, remembers Jeff from the class. He recalls that Jeff was evasive about his plans. Many of the participants would have meals together, sometimes talking about subjects they didn't want to raise in class. At one meal, Howorth asked Jeff what he wanted to do after the course. "I'm not really sure," he lied. It wasn't that unusual, since many of the students were reluctant to give away information that might tip off a competitor, such as where they wanted to open their store.

On the last day of class, Howorth said goodbye to Jeff. "I said, 'I'm not really sure what you're going to do, but I have a feeling you'll be successful.'" What led him to that conclusion? "I could

64

tell he was bright and quick," says Howorth. "I had no real idea, but the way he was deeply mysterious about it, I could tell he was doing some deep thinking about it, a lot of planning. And he had a very friendly smile."

Howorth had no idea that the smiling Jeff who took his course would become a major competitor of virtually every bookstore on earth—until a few years later at an American Booksellers Association conference. "I saw Jeff and recognized his face, but I was not sure from where," he recalls. "Maybe someone from my hometown? I asked him how he was doing. Then I looked at his shirt, and it said Amazon.com. I suddenly knew exactly who he was. I said, 'Oh, my God, it's you!' I didn't know *Jeff Bezos* had been in the class."

With an introductory course in bookselling, some experience buying a few items online, one computer, two engineers, his wife, and a garage, Bezos was ready to start building an online bookstore.

Chapter 6

How to Build a Better Bookstore

We used to joke that the ideal Amazon site would not show a search box, navigation links, or lists of things you could buy. Instead, it would just display a giant picture of one book, the next book you want to buy.

—Greg Linden, former Amazon programmer

I t took Jeff Bezos and his tiny team just one year to go from settling into Seattle to launching a company. First, he had to get some computers to run his site and store all the data he had collected about books. He bought two or three Sun Microsystem workstations, small but powerful computers often used by engineers to design products or run computer networks.

Amazon's biggest expense was obviously going to be buying or building software. Start-up executives often make the mistake of assuming no outsiders can build software as well as their own programmers. They end up wasting time and money building what they could have easily bought from a vendor that had already worked out the bugs and refined its programs.

Bezos, however, knew what he was doing. He probably knew as much about programming as the people he had hired to do it for him. He carefully chose what to buy and what to build. In order to run the basic operations of the company and manage all the data, he and his programmers chose Oracle Corporation's Oracle database management system. It's an expensive system, but well tested, reliable, and widely used by giant corporations to store and manage their data. In fact, it was more powerful than the tiny company needed at the time. But Bezos had confidence in his future, and Oracle's software would allow the company to grow without having to switch systems. Davis and Kaphan were careful to keep that issue in mind when writing their own software as well. They didn't want to be replacing systems as the company grew, another common problem with start-up companies. "Jeff was very concerned about scaling the company," says Peri Hartman.

Still, Oracle was a general-purpose system. Amazon's software designers had to build upon it to do exactly what the company wanted. In that process, the programmers made a lot of mistakes. Kaphan was primarily responsible for the Web site software that would be seen and used by customers, while Davis focused mostly on the back-end systems that conducted transactions and ran the company. Neither Davis nor Kaphan were experts in relational database systems. "We made some good guesses and a lot of poor ones," Davis would later say.

But the team still had to build a lot of software themselves. Executive hubris? Probably not. This team was building an unusual company of a type that had never really existed before. Since they had to spend time creating their own programs, they did it on the cheap.

In order to keep costs down, they relied heavily on open source software, free programs such as the UNIX operating system and the C and Perl programming languages, all of which were able to run on the Sun workstations Bezos had bought. Open source software is built by hobbyists and university professors and students, is widely distributed, and can be enhanced or added to by anyone. The open source strategy, in fact, became popular for many other dot-com companies, including Google. Although Amazon's programmers had no experience in retail, back-office, or customer-centric software, Jeff got his stock options' worth from them. They *were* familiar with open source programs, allowing them to create the workhorse software they needed. Davis and Kaphan built their software on top of the free UNIX operating system using the free programming languages.

In addition to the Oracle system that would manage the database program, they had to build their own database that would hold all the information to run the company. So they made it from an open source system called DBM (database manager), which had been created at AT&T and later improved upon by the University of California at Berkeley and others. That required modifying it to make it run on UNIX. When the company launched in 1995, its overall database of books contained more than a million titles, requiring more than two gigabytes of memory. They put the thousand most popular books into a twenty-five-megabyte computer memory system that could respond very quickly to requests through the DBM program.

With a database containing more than a million books, Jeff

began to claim that Amazon was "the biggest bookstore on earth." That was a nice marketing gimmick of questionable veracity. For one, Bezos didn't want his company to have any inventory—or, at least, he wanted the inventory to pass through his hands very quickly, in and out the same day. What he actually had was a huge database of book titles and information about them. His plan was to order the books from publishers or distributors only after his customers had ordered them from him (a goal he later had to abandon as Amazon grew). His belief was that Amazon would then be able to operate with much lower overhead than physical bookstores and mail-order companies. Another reason the claim of a million books was an exaggeration is that even the distributors had only about 300,000 books in stock at any one time. In another sleight of hand, although Bezos claimed Amazon to be a bookstore with 1.1 million titles, his database actually had a list of 1.5 million titles. One source later told book author Robert Spector that the reason for the lowball figure was so that Amazon could later claim 1.5 million books, making it seem as though the inventory had grown.

In terms of the number of books actually on hand at any one time, Amazon's competitors could have just as easily described it as one of the smallest bookstores on earth. In fact, any physical bookstore could claim access to just as many titles as Amazon, because that bookstore could order any books from distributors or publishers just as Amazon did. The difference was that Amazon could find the titles quickly in its custom-built database and place the orders faster than a physical bookstore could using people staffing a help desk.

Amazon's programmers still had to create a highly customized inventory tracking system, because the company still had to keep track of books moving from the publisher or distributor to Amazon's warehouse and then to the customer. Since mail-order companies did keep books in stock, they typically had only two categories for inventory: in stock or on back order. Bezos wanted more precision, so Davis had to write an inventory tracking system specifically for Amazon. If Amazon already had a copy in its warehouse, the book was listed as able to ship in one day. If a distributor had a book in stock, it was promised in two or three days. (If nearby Ingram had it, the book could often make it out in one day.) If a book had to be ordered from a publisher, delivery to the customer might take a week or two. If the book was out of stock at both the publisher and distributors, it was listed as "shipped in four to six weeks or maybe never." Books that were out of print fell into the "maybe never" category. (Bezos would still try to find the out-of-print books, and sometimes managed to do so from publishers or other bookstores, a feature that gave Amazon a reputation early on as an amazing place to find books.) The general strategy was to be conservative when estimating when a book would be shipped, so that surprises would be positive—shipped sooner than the customer expected—rather than negative.

Still, some of the tasks had to be done by hand and were extraordinarily tedious. That meant a lot of work for Bezos's tiny team of programmers. In order to find books, for example, Amazon used a database of titles called *Books in Print*, published by R. R. Bowker, which lists all in-print books by their International Standard Book Number (ISBN). It provided this list—a million and a half titles altogether—to publishers, bookstores, and libraries on CD-ROM disks. Getting the lists into Amazon's computers was like moving a giant pile of sand with a teaspoon, because Amazon did not have the huge, expensive computers used by large corporations to suck up the data quickly. The programmers could only transfer six hundred books at a time, which meant someone had to copy and paste blocks of titles twenty-five hundred times to copy an entire disk. R. R. Bowker sent out an updated disk every week, and just transferring the updates took almost an entire day.

Different databases of books were not always reliable, however. They often had different data about which books were available. So the Amazon team determined which were more reliable with a simple test: They would order books and see which databases were accurate. They found that when distributors or publishers claimed that books were out of stock, they were often actually out of print. But when they acknowledged that a book was out of print, that was usually the truth.

The next problem was how to take orders from customers and collect the money from them. That was a new issue for the Internet, which had just recently opened up for commerce. The Amazon brains didn't know if people would be comfortable placing orders and giving credit card numbers over the Internet, or if they would prefer to use email, or to call the company directly, or to simply mail in a check. There were already well-publicized cases of hackers breaking into the files of Internet companies and stealing credit card information. The most obvious solution was to provide for every scenario.

At first, the team thought email was the most likely scenario to work, since email users outnumbered Internet users by ten to one. So they created an email ordering system: A customer could search for a book on the site, but the rest could be handled by email, on the assumption that people would be more comfortable with it: placing the order by email, getting an email back letting them know how soon it could be shipped, then sending a credit card number back via email.

By the time Amazon opened for business, the petri dish of the Internet had become so popular that the email system wasn't needed, and Amazon was able to rely mostly on orders coming directly through the Web site. About half the customers phoned in their credit card numbers, and some paid by check, but the team was surprised that a significant number of customers were willing to do the transactions directly through the Web site.

Of course, that meant that keeping the credit card numbers safe was of paramount importance. Davis created that system, something he dubbed the "CC Motel," a play on Black Flag's Roach Motel, where "roaches check in, but they don't check out." Credit card numbers could be entered into the system, but hackers would not be able to get them out. The approach was simple: Never put the credit card information into any computer that was connected to the Internet. The card number was transferred to a floppy disk and walked over to the transaction processing computer. (In those early days of unreliable computer networks, companies called this a "sneaker-net" network, a backup for when they couldn't get the network to function properly.) The CC Motel computer was connected by a telephone-based modem only to the credit card companies and to the book distributors, and was used both for charging the credit cards and for ordering the books from the distributors. The books were ordered first, in order to make sure they were available. Only then were the credit cards charged.

This early system worked, although it was almost laughably

simplistic, and was one that would obviously have to be replaced once orders reached substantial levels. Davis later recalled that he would have nightmares about the system. The data was supposed to be backed up onto another computer every night, but the team would sometimes forget to do it. Sometimes they lost or accidentally wrote over files that might contain a couple hundred transactions. That required going back to the CC Motel and printing out a list of the credit card numbers, then calling the credit card company to go through the numbers one at a time to make sure the transactions had been processed. At other times, they lost files of credit card numbers and would have to get the credit card company to fax back a list of the transactions, which contained only the last four digits of the credit cards, and someone at Amazon would have to sit down with the list and match them to their list of transactions. "We didn't take seriously the responsibility of keeping that data in a good state," said Davis.

But there were also features of the shopping site that few other companies thought to build in, features that gave customers confidence in using the system. For example, people did not have to even register with the site in order to start looking for books or putting them into a shopping basket. "We let people get well into the ordering process before we made them create an account, which was a real stumbling block on some other early e-commerce sites," says Kaphan.

In order to assuage customers' fears about leaving their credit card information online, Jeff's mandate was to make the ordering process "gentle," as Kaphan puts it. So they were given the option of leaving just the last few digits of their credit card number, and calling in the full number by phone when they were ready to be charged. And Amazon made sure that the customers knew they would not be charged until the very last step, eliminating the fear that they would buy a book accidentally. "Users were always reassured at each step that they were not making irreversible steps until they were ready to commit their orders," says Kaphan. "I remember that next to the button to put something in the shopping basket, I put something like 'you can always take it out later.'"

This was all part of Bezos's mandate to make sure the site was the best around, a philosophy that the programmers took very seriously. The Web was new, confusing, and more than a bit intimidating to most people, and generating trust was (and still is) highly valued online. The Amazon.com system helped meet Bezos's goal of creating a good experience for customers. Mainly, he knew that this approach was key to the company's success.

In fact, Davis and Kaphan were not only able to make the site trustworthy and easy to use, they made it more useful than shopping off-line. Any good Web site should exploit the technology of computers and the Internet to do things that can't be done off-line. Very few of the early dot-com companies figured out how to do that. But Bezos reasoned that if customers can get the same service off-line, why change to a new medium that seems confusing or even scary? "The Web is an infant technology," Bezos said at the time. "If you want to be successful in the short-to-medium term, you can only do things that offer incredibly strong value propositions to customers relative to the value of doing things in more traditional ways. This basically means that, right now, you should only do on-line what you cannot do any other way."

Amazon's programmers found a way to offer something that can't be done off-line by making it easy to tap the company's database in order to find information about books and authors. Kaphan tapped his expertise in creating hypertext, or links from one piece of data to another. He and Davis took all the biographical information about authors in the Amazon database and intertwined it through links. Customers were able to search through all subjects and authors they found of interest. If they found one book they liked, they could click on the author's name and find all the other books he or she had written. They could click on a subject category to find other books on that subject. Who needs a Dewey Decimal System? "I always thought that the hypertextualization of the bibliographic information was key [to Amazon's early success]," says Kaphan. "You could navigate through the large space of available books."

Aside from weeding out the bugs in the internal workings of the site, Amazon's programmers had to make sure the site would work properly with several different Web browsers, each with different features. The graphical browser was what made the Internet popular, by turning it into a simple point-and-click navigation system. In the early days of the Internet, nobody could be sure which Web browser would be most popular.

University students from around the world were cranking out graphical browsers to take advantage of the World Wide Web communications standards developed by Tim Berners-Lee at the European Organization for Nuclear Research in the suburbs of Geneva. Some of the earliest graphical browsers from the early 1990s were now largely forgotten or overlooked names like Erwise, developed at the Helsinki University of Technology; ViolaWWW, from the University of California, Berkeley; and Lynx, created at the University of Kansas.

But the one that really got people moving to the Internet was Mosaic, developed at the Urbana-Champaign campus of the University of Illinois, in the school's famed National Center for Supercomputing Applications (NCSA). It was the foundation for the Netscape Navigator, the first successful commercial browser (although offered for free), created at Netscape Communications by former Illinois students who had worked on the Mosaic browser. By 1995, Netscape also had competition from Microsoft's Internet Explorer, which ended up capturing most of the market.

By the spring of 1995, Amazon had a Web site. The site wasn't finished yet, but it was working well enough to let a few hundred friends try it out—after they were sworn to secrecy, of course. With the promise not to tell anyone about the project, the beta testers began browsing through books and making pretend purchases.

One problem Amazon's programmers discovered during testing was that there was no way to track an individual customer's activity. If someone bought a book, then started browsing for other items, Amazon's computers had no way of knowing that both actions were done by the same person. It's one of those things you don't realize you need until you discover you don't have it. They had to build in a system that would store all activity from a particular user into one file, and pull out that data when a customer returned.

Some of the site's important features just reflected a lack of resources. The programmers used few graphics in the early days, mainly because they didn't have many to work with. They were not graphic designers, and many book publishers were either unable or unwilling to supply them with images. But that turned out be a feature customers liked. Internet connections were very slow in those days, and graphics took a long time to download. Also, some of the early Web browsers were text-only, unable to display graphics, so Kaphan and Davis made sure all the necessary information was provided without the need for images. Just try turning off the graphics in a Web browser today and you'll see how many critical pieces of information and links disappear from most sites.

Again, many early dot-com companies missed the point. They put as many graphic images as possible on their sites (and many still do) under the mistaken belief that it makes their sites look more professional or their ads more noticeable. In reality, the sites just become more annoying and confusing. In fact, Google was later to stumble on this same approach, demonstrating that a spare Web site is still vastly superior to one flashing images and shouting out sound effects like a late-night TV pitchman selling $19.95 items not available in stores.

Bezos had to improvise to deal with unexpected problems, and he did so with élan, if not a devious glee. For instance, he wanted to test his ordering systems to make sure they worked properly and to work out bugs. That meant ordering one book at a time. But the distributors wanted a minimum order of ten books. He was later to say in his speeches that he had offered to pay the distributors extra to get just one book, but they refused to break procedure. Bezos discovered, however, that if some books in a particular order weren't in stock, the distributors would still ship the others and charge for only the books shipped. He then found an obscure book on lichens that both distributors supposedly carried, but did not actually have in stock. So in order to run his tests, he started placing orders for the one book he wanted, plus nine of the lichen books. "They would deliver the one that we wanted, along with a

—

very sincere apology about not having been able to fulfill the nine copies of the lichen book order," he said. "That worked very well for exercising our systems. I've since talked and joked at length with the people at these companies about this. They actually think it's very funny."

In many ways, Amazon's early design was a combination of trial and error, good guessing, chance, and some clever improvisation. But the small team kept an eye on what was important: giving priority to the customers' needs rather than trying to extract every dollar possible from their virtual wallets. They paid attention to what customers liked and what they didn't. That approach gave Amazon a good start—and continued to be a guiding beacon in the company's future.

Chapter 7

Growing Pains

Amazon.com was finally launched on July 16, 1995. It was just in time—just as masses of people started moving onto the Internet and before many competitors had created good commercial sites. Amazon.com was launched with the latest technology and cleanest design in the middle of the year when Internet use grew several times, to sixteen million people. Bezos was able to take advantage of his observation of bacterialike growth online to get an early start on competitors. That fortuitous timing was a key piece of luck and hard work from the programmers.

Bezos was also able to move his company out of his altered garage. He set up shop in an industrial neighborhood in Seattle that he shared with a needle exchange and a shuttered pawnshop. He had eleven hundred square feet of office space on the second floor and four hundred square feet in the basement to be used as a warehouse. The desks were made from cheap doors with sawed-off two-by-fours for legs. (As Amazon grew, Bezos hired a carpentry firm in Seattle to build them for $130—$70 for materials and

$60 for labor.) One room of the office space was used to store card-
board boxes. The CC Motel and Internet computers sat on a cheap
metal shelf. The warehouse held more shelves to store just a few
hundred books on their way from the distributor to the customer,
a couple of tables with supplies to pack up books for shipments,
a metered scale, and a Pitney Bowes postage machine. He also
placed whiteboards in the elevators so employees could scribble
ideas during some of the only free time they managed to squeeze
into their days.

Orders started coming in as soon as the site launched. In the
first few days, there were half a dozen orders per day. One of the
programmers set up a program so that every computer at Amazon
would ring a bell every time an order came in. A great novelty at
first, it quickly got too annoying and had to be turned off after a
few days.

Discounted books, of course, were the first big draw to Amazon's site. When the site first launched in 1995, Bezos put everything on sale. The top twenty or so best-selling books were sold at
30 percent below list price, which meant Bezos was selling them
as loss leaders. This is a practice often used by the big bookstore
chains. (Perhaps Bezos learned that in his bookselling class.) But
Bezos also cut the price of all three hundred thousand titles that
the distributors had in stock by 10 percent.

The staff picked out a special selection of books for the daily
Spotlight, chosen partly by how much information was available
to add as a Spotlight profile, and discounted them by up to 40 percent. With these discounts, Amazon could beat the prices of even
the big chain stores.

The fact that Bezos managed to get online before the big bookstore chains was an invaluable advantage. A huge number of those early Internet users were the famed "early adopters" of new technology that all tech companies covet. The early adopters found Amazon.com, decided it was good, and word spread throughout the Internet. After that, it was hard for any other bookseller, no matter how good, to match Amazon's cachet.

Three days after launch, Bezos got an email from Jerry Yang, one of the founders of Yahoo. "Jerry said, 'We think your site is pretty cool; would you like us to put it on the What's Cool page?'" Bezos recalled. "We thought about it some, and we realized it might be like taking a sip from a fire hose, but we decided to go ahead and go for it." Yahoo put the site on the list, and orders soared. By the end of the week, Amazon took in over $12,000 worth of orders. It was hard to keep up. That week, the company shipped just $846 worth of books. The following week brought in nearly $15,000 worth of orders, and the team was able to ship just over $7,000 worth of the orders.

The site wasn't even truly finished when the company launched. Bezos's philosophy was to get to market quickly to get a lead on the competition, and fix problems and improve the site as people started using it. One mistake they discovered after launch: People could put a negative number into the box that asked how many copies of the book they were ordering. "We found that customers could order a negative quantity of books!" Bezos later recalled. "And we would credit their credit card with the price and, I assume, wait around for them to ship the books."

Another mistake was that Bezos had not hired anyone to pack

up and ship the products as they arrived from the distributors. The first few weeks, everyone at the company was working until two or three in the morning to get them packed, addressed, and shipped.

Bezos had also neglected to order packing tables, so people ended up on their knees on the concrete floor to package the books. He later recalled in a speech to Lake Forest College that, after hours on his knees packing up books, he commented to one of the employees that they had to get knee pads. The employee, Nicholas Lovejoy, "looked at me like I was a Martian," Bezos recalled with a laugh. Lovejoy suggested the obvious: Buy some tables. "I thought that was the most brilliant idea I had ever heard in my life!" Bezos finally went to the Home Depot and splurged on some tables.

The company was strictly a cut-rate operation. Any printing or copying was done at a Print Mart shop a few blocks away. Business meetings were held at a local coffee shop—ironically, one inside a Barnes & Noble bookstore. Employees bought the office supplies they needed and submitted an invoice at the end of the month to be reimbursed. All employees, including Bezos, answered emails from customers with questions, comments, or complaints.

Despite what seemed to be a pathetically amateurish operation, Amazon grew up very quickly once it was launched. By October, Amazon had its first day logging in one hundred book sales. In less than a year, it had its first hour with an order of one hundred books. Word kept spreading, despite the fact that the company did no advertising its first year—although Bezos did hire mobile billboards to cruise by Barnes & Noble stores displaying the question, "Can't find that book you wanted?" along with Amazon's Web site address.

Word spread through the Internet. Netscape put the site on

its "What's New" list, and many other sites did the same. Amazon was always near the top of the lists because the lists were mostly alphabetical—exactly why Bezos chose a name that began with an A. Even *The Wall Street Journal* ran an article about the tiny company on its front page. That got traffic soaring. "It was also a curse, because it alerted our competitors—of which there were many and large—to our existence," Bezos recalled. "In particular, Barnes & Noble started to take notice of what we were doing." About a year later, in May 1996, Barnes & Noble launched its online bookstore, about a week before Amazon's initial public offering.

But Bezos prepared himself for the competition. He kept adding features that kept the competition a step behind no matter how fast they ran. Although virtually all the customer service features would later be automated, in the early days everything had to be done with human intervention. In the daily Spotlight, Amazon editors highlighted certain books with extra information and reviews. When publishers failed to provide sufficient information about a book the editors wanted to spotlight, they started writing their own, even if it meant visiting a nearby bookstore and scribbling down notes from a dust jacket.

Soon, Amazon's human editors were recommending books to customers based on similar purchases they had made in the past. They might alert, say, Cormac McCarthy fans that their favorite author had released a new book, or American history fans that the latest edition of *The Civil War Battle Guide* had arrived. These were all the kind of services once reserved for regular patrons of local bookstores with knowledgeable staffs.

But Bezos was also determined to add features that would be difficult or impossible for physical bookstores to put in place.

The Internet offers two-way communications, and Bezos realized that he could get his customers to do some of the editorial work themselves, while indulging their passion for books and their desire to pontificate. Amazon invited readers to offer their own reviews, had other customers rate the reviews, and asked authors to answer questions posted online by readers. The company also allowed people to visit the site as "visible" or "invisible." With the former option, people browsing the same category of books could communicate with each other and recommend books they liked. In one terrific publicity stunt, John Updike started a short story titled "Murder Makes the Magazine" for the site and asked readers to submit additions to the story. That brought in four hundred thousand endings for the story. For six weeks, Amazon chose a weekly winner from the selections and awarded them $1,000. From those six, a final winner was randomly chosen for a $100,000 prize. Amazon wasn't just a selling site; it became an early social network site for book fans.

This feedback from customers was originally controversial. They were allowed to write bad reviews of books, and competitors couldn't understand why a bookseller would allow such a thing. Who would buy a book that someone panned? Some local bookstores have employees write reviews of books they like, but they just ignore books they don't like. It was all part of Jeff's plan "to create the world's most consumer-centric company." Within a few weeks after starting the customer review process, he has said, "I started receiving letters from well-meaning folks saying that perhaps you don't understand your business. You make money when you sell things. Why are you allowing negative reviews on your Web site? But our point of view is we will sell more if we help people make purchasing decisions."

These tactics worked partly because they were such unusual moves. Customer reviews and recommendations taught people that Amazon was a different kind of store, one that could be relied upon to point out books that were probably a waste of time and money. It helped build up goodwill. It reinforced Bezos's image as an executive who actually cared about his customers.

This was an important example of Bezos's attempt to fully take advantage of the Internet, to do things online that couldn't be done in a physical store. Strangers don't generally start recommending books to each other in a bookstore. "I'm an outgoing person, but I'd never go into a bookstore and ask a complete stranger to recommend a book," Bezos has said. "The semi-anonymity of the online environment makes people less inhibited." Amazon also started "redecorating" the store for each customer, calling up books in genres people had expressed interest in, or recommending books based on past buying patterns. "These interactive features are going to be incredibly powerful," Bezos predicted in 1996. "And you can't reproduce them in the physical world. Physical stores have to be designed for the lowest common denominator."

Research and feedback from customers indicated that selection and convenience were very important to them. In order to improve those features, Bezos worked on developing much stronger relationships with the book distributors. In the summer of 1996 there were no written contracts with the distributors, and no one to ensure deliveries were running smoothly. The ordering department was made up of one employee and two PCs. Amazon had no one in charge of returning books to distributors when they didn't sell, and many of them were backing up on shelves. So Bezos hired some people to take over and get it organized. In six months, the company went from ordering a hundred books a day to ordering five thousand.

Another important talent Bezos has always displayed is a willingness to jump on new ideas that come from any source. One clever idea came from one of his customers. In July 1996, the company got a request from someone who liked recommending books on her own Web site. She asked for permission to link those reviews to the corresponding books on Amazon, so people could buy them. Bezos realized that this could be a big boost to his business. So the company created its Associates Program, inviting businesses and other organizations to link to books in Amazon's database. Whenever someone clicked on that link and bought a book on Amazon, the associated site would get a commission of 5 to 15 percent on the sale, depending on the item sold.

Aside from the revenues it brought in, the program proved to be a big boon to Amazon's reputation as a site where enthusiasts of any subject could find books they wanted. Since a site for, say, fans of classic Mustang cars could link to books on the subject, the idea that Amazon could find any book on any topic grew. In 1998, Bezos described the program as "one of the most innovative things that we have done." The idea of the Associates Program was also patented by Amazon.

This patent also became controversial, with claims that it was already being done elsewhere on the Internet. Sites often linked to other sites where people could make purchases, sometimes even collecting a fee for the referral. But Bezos argued that his approach was different. The Associate sites were essentially mini virtual bookstores themselves, using Amazon's technology to locate the books and buy them. The other difference was that it was a broad program for which anybody could sign up without negotiating deals with Amazon, or even talking to anyone at the company first. The patent was granted several years later, but Bezos never sued anybody for creating their own affiliate programs, the practice spread, and the controversy faded away.

Still, this is the kind of program that many executives find abhorrent. In 1997, for example, Microsoft's Sidewalk sites, which listed things to do in town, started linking to the page on Ticketmaster's site where people could buy a ticket to a particular event. Ticketmaster sued. Ticketmaster executives wanted Microsoft to pay for the privelege of sending buyers to the site and, when Microsoft turned them down, managed to get a paying deal with competitor Citysearch. For Microsoft, Ticketmaster would only allow links to its home page, despite the inconvenience to customers.

Ticketmaster was widely derided by Internet pundits for its counterproductive self-serving attitude. Two years later, Microsoft gave in and agreed to link only to Ticketmaster's home page.

And yet, some sites are still resistant to allowing other Web sites to send people their way, even though those people might be paying customers or actually interested in the sites' ads. Most of the reluctance comes from news sites that complain about search engines giving news summaries along with links to the original stories, even though it is well documented that the links vastly increase traffic to the news sites and boost their ratings in search engines. People like News Corporation's Rupert Murdoch keep threatening to sue Google for putting teasers of News Corporation articles on Google News and linking back to the original source.

By not only accepting the practice, but actually paying other sites to provide links, Bezos demonstrated the difference between an entrepreneur embracing the Internet and its unique capabilities, and older executives who didn't understand the new medium and only reluctantly joined the virtual world. Fueled by that understanding, Bezos started moving even faster in the race to the top of the dot-com heap.

Chapter 8

Money to Burn Through

We know two percent today. I think Amazon.com may know as much as any other company about e-commerce, but I bet you we know two percent of what we will know 10 years from now. This is the *Kitty Hawk* era of e-commerce, and most of the interesting stuff hasn't even begun to be invented yet.

—Jeff Bezos, 1998

Amazon's growth was stellar in its first year and a half. But it was still limited by a shortage of cash. Like most young companies, Amazon was losing money. Bezos was focused not just on keeping up with the growth that seemed to be coming so easily, but on setting up the organization to quickly become profitable. That meant he had to spend judiciously and to keep his boldest ambitions in check.

By the time the company launched in the summer of 1995, Bezos had to start raising more money. He had run through the cash he and his family could contribute. That's when he called his friend Nick Hanauer, who had said he wanted to invest and helped convince Bezos to start his company in Seattle. Hanauer started making calls to people around Seattle who had money—some of them from the sale of their Microsoft stock. But there was a problem. Although Hanauer was impressed with Bezos, he said Bezos was terrible at convincing potential investors "how smart he was, how accomplished he was, and how focused he was." That meant trouble, because the idea of an online bookstore sounded to most people like little more than a novelty in 1995, despite the buzz being generated online.

Sure enough, it was hard to raise the money, although some of the investors have said they were impressed with Bezos's intelligence. One potential investor didn't seem impressed with Bezos's enthusiasm about petri-dish growth, because everyone kept telling him that people loved going into bookstores and did not want to buy online. But Bezos could recite an extraordinary amount of statistics from his research, and it eventually made a difference. A Seattle-based Smith Barney stockbroker named Eric Dillon was interested in investing, but thought that the valuation Bezos had put on the company—$6 million—was pulled out of thin air, until Bezos sat down with him to show how much other Internet companies were trying to raise. Dillon talked Bezos down to a $5 million valuation, and put in some money. A prominent Seattle businessman named Tom Alberg was impressed with Bezos's projections that Amazon could turn over the equivalent of an average bookstore's inventory 20 times a year, compared to 2.7 times for most bookstores—with details to lend credibility to the claim.

In the end, Hanauer managed to get some commitments by making the first investment himself. Others followed, and by the end of the year another twenty investors kicked in money, most of them around $30,000 apiece. Bezos raised $981,000. In order to add more management talent to the company, Bezos brought investors Nick Hanauer, Eric Dillon, and Tom Alberg in as advisers to the company.

Then, in 1996, the tide changed with a roar. Wall Street was starting to catch Internet fever. Millions of new users were getting online every year. Furthermore, Netscape had stoked the investment fires with its spectacular IPO in August 1995. So in early 1996, the inevitable happened. A venture capitalist called Jeff Bezos.

Ramanan Raghavendran was surfing the Internet one day, and happened to hit upon Amazon.com. Raghavendran was responsible for finding Internet investments for General Atlantic, an investment firm in Connecticut. He was impressed with what he heard from Bezos in their phone conversation, and wanted to put in some money at a valuation of about $10 million—twice what the company had been valued at in its private round of funding just a few months earlier.

Bezos did not jump at the offer. Instead, it got him thinking. Just how much interest would there be from the venture capitalist community? How much money could he raise if he got serious about it? Amazon was approaching an annual revenue run rate of $5 million, and growth was getting faster all the time. Forget the idea of giving the company a total value of $10 million, Bezos and his advisers started thinking about raising $50 million for just part of the company. They went shopping for investors.

One thing Bezos has never lacked is faith in himself, even if others didn't always share that view in Amazon's early days. So he went straight to the top. His advisory board and some of his employees had connections at Kleiner Perkins Caufield & Byers, so people started making calls to probably the top venture capitalist in Silicon Valley, KPCB's John Doerr.

Doerr didn't return their phone calls. But other venture capitalists did. It was the precursor to the dot-com era, when any business plan that incorporated the Internet into its model was starting to look like it was written on gold. Bezos and his advisers got cocky. They decided that, with an offer from General Atlantic on the table, they could take the time to find the best deal. They researched other venture capitalist firms, but still liked KPCB best. Bezos talked to other companies that KPCB had invested in, both successes and failures, and wanted John Doerr and his company behind him.

The team met with General Atlantic again. Dillon let the potential investors talk for an hour and half before saying anything. Finally, they looked at him, and he put some very high cards on the table. "We're only willing to sign a deal with you guys today if you're willing to give us a valuation of $100 million." The General Atlantic team was stunned. Dillon admitted that he and Bezos came up with that number because it was a "staggering, outrageous stop-us-in-our-track number." The plan was to just see how high they could go, while researching other venture capitalists. "Afterwards, Jeff and I went out to dinner and we just laughed all night long about their reactions. In the annals of Amazon, it was just a really fun day."

General Atlantic returned later with an offer that would value the company at $50 million. Bezos and Dillon turned it down. Then the offer was upped to a valuation between $60 million and $70 million. Negotiations started getting serious.

Finally, though, someone from KPCB did call Bezos. Bezos acted cool and said Doerr should travel to Seattle to meet with him. The fact that there was already a good offer on the table allowed Bezos to play hardball. KPCB offered $8 million for 13 percent of the company's stock, giving it a valuation of $60 million. Bezos demanded that Doerr join the company's board as part of the investment. Doerr held out for a while, but finally gave in because there was so much interest from others. Although Amazon might have gotten a better valuation from General Atlantic, Bezos felt that Doerr's name was worth the extra $10 million he might have gotten in valuation. In the spring of 1996 he took the offer. Despite the fact that others have said that Bezos was determined to get Doerr and KPCB from the start, his hardball tactics with the company worked. "We had to compete like crazy for the right to invest in Amazon," Doerr was later to say.

Now Bezos was playing with real money. With that, his strategy changed. He had been planning to make the company profitable quickly so that he could either bootstrap operations or attract serious investors, but he had now done that without profits. So he decided that rather than trying to run the company at a profit, he would invest heavily in more people, new technologies, and new market opportunities. It was now a race: Whoever captured market share first would establish the pole position and would be difficult to pass. The mandate now was, "Get big fast."

He made no secret about the strategy. "We are not profitable," he told *The New York Times* in January 1997. "We could be. It would be the easiest thing in the world to be profitable. It would also be the dumbest. We are taking what might be profits and reinvesting them in the future of the business. It would literally be the stupidest decision any management team could make to make Amazon.com profitable right now."

That didn't mean he became profligate with his cash. Anticipating competition from much better-funded bookstore chains like Borders and Barnes & Noble, he spent money on things that would give Amazon an advantage. He moved Amazon into larger facilities, but stuck to his door-desks. At a 1997 picnic, in order to promote the idea of growing quickly on a minimal budget, Bezos handed out T-shirts silkscreened with a blazing sun, the center of which held a hot dog and the words "Get Big Fast . . . Have Another Hot Dog!" And that's exactly what the Amazonians were fed.

Bezos didn't have to rely on the KPCB money for very long. On May 14, 1997, just one year after getting his venture capitalist investment and less than two years after opening the doors for business, he took Amazon public at $18 per share, raising another $54 million and valuing the company at $429 million. At any other time in history, that would have been outrageous. When the company first announced plans for its IPO two months earlier, analysts thought his initial plan to sell stock for up to $13 per share for a $300 million valuation was crazy. But this was the early stage of Internet fever. Bill Bass, an analyst at Forrester Research, insisted the valuation was way too high. "Some people smoke Internet inhalant and their judgment gets bizarre," Bass said. Of course, this was the same firm that dubbed the company Amazon.toast.

Investors in the IPO didn't seem worried about Amazon's lack of profitability. The IPO prospectus spelled out the strategy and the risk clearly. Not only was Amazon unprofitable, it said, "The rate at which such losses will be incurred will increase significantly from current levels, and its recent revenue growth rates are not sustainable and will decrease in the future." Bezos then kept his word to remain unprofitable by slashing the price of four hundred thousand of Amazon's books by up to 40 percent in order to keep the superstores from making inroads online.

But Bezos couldn't just ignore the bookselling superstores. Barnes & Noble had sued the company to stop it from advertising that it was "the world's largest bookstore," since Amazon carried relatively little inventory itself. Bezos countersued, claiming that Barnes & Noble did not deserve the privilege of selling books without charging sales tax, since that right was reserved for online sales to customers in states where the company had no physical presence, while the company had physical bookstores in almost all states in the United States. The companies later settled their suits without disclosing any terms.

One year after the IPO, Amazon's stock was selling for $105 per share, valuing the company at $5 billion, more than the valuations of Barnes & Noble and Borders combined. It had lost another $30 million since the IPO. So why were investors so ready to put money behind this apparently shaky company? Amazon had become the premier Internet commerce site. With a two-year head start over the competition, huge brand name recognition, and growth in revenues, it had become an Internet star. It also had low inventory and pulled in $300,000 in sales per employee, more than three times the revenue-per-employee rate of physical bookstores. Plus, Bezos was holding on to 41 percent of the company's shares himself, with KPCB holding another 12 percent (its holding had been diluted since its investment), so high demand drove up the price of a relatively hard-to-get stock.

But mostly, people had come to love the site. The famous Jeff

Bezos attention to detail and performance had paid off. The view of Amazon was described by *Time* magazine a month before the IPO: "The site is so fast and responsive it almost feels alive; it's thrilling to have every title in the language at your fingertips, and reader-produced reviews add a layer of egalitarian interactivity."

Growing quickly without even trying to turn a profit became the mantra for virtually all other Internet companies that followed, the strategy that defined the dot-com era of the late 1990s. For most it didn't work. Netscape was trying the same strategy, but was later sideswiped by Microsoft, which had much deeper pockets. The dot-com companies collapsed when the market crashed in 2000 and 2001, unable to reach profitability. But Bezos played the strategy just right. Amazon became the first Internet company to completely redefine an industry.

Chapter 9

Growing Up

Changing an industry requires a lot more than a great idea. It requires a thousand new ideas, near-flawless execution, and a lot of guts. Once he had secured his venture capital funding, Bezos started adding features to the Web site and hiring new people like a kid collecting Halloween candy. In September 1997 he added the 1-Click shopping feature. Five months later he decided to offer other bookstores the opportunity to sell through Amazon on consignment with the Advantage Program, giving small, independent bookstores access to Amazon's formidable online presence.

He also pushed advertising heavily in order to get the company's name beyond the technology elite, the early adopters of Internet technology. According to Jupiter Communications, he spent more than $340,000 in the first half of 1996, and ranked thirty-fourth in Web ad spending. He set up multiyear advertising agreements with Internet portals including Yahoo, Excite, and AOL. He hired a Silicon Valley ad agency, USWeb/CKS, which came up with a series of memorable ads designed to show the breadth of Amazon's offerings in a humorous way: "163 books on marriage, 798 books on divorce"; "16 books on male pattern baldness, 128 on hats"; "460 books for Marxists, including 33 on Groucho."

By mid-1998 he was spending over $26 million on marketing in just three months, running ads both online and in major newspapers such as *The New York Times* and *The Wall Street Journal*, then moving into radio and cable news shows such as CNN. By the end of 1998, he was spending nearly a quarter of his revenues just on advertising. Today Amazon is a huge advertiser—it spent nearly $600 million on advertising and promotion in 2009.

Hiring went into high gear. By late 1996 there were a hundred and ten employees, fourteen of them dedicated to answering emails from customers. Some of the new hires had little to do at first. "He had hired more managers even though they weren't needed yet," says early Amazon programmer Peri Hartman. "They might have just a couple people reporting to them. But it gave them time to get to know the company. He let them be managers before they had to handle a large number of people." Some of the new hires in key positions even had previous experience that applied to their new jobs: marketing, project management, distribution, finance, even an executive from Barnes & Noble.

And Bezos managed to hire only the best. The interview process for new hires was as demanding as going through oral exams for a Ph.D. in subparticle physics. Each candidate would go through interviews with several employees, then with Jeff, who would also grill all the other interviewers. He would create elaborate charts on a whiteboard listing the candidate's qualifications, and rejected anyone about whom he had the slightest doubt. References were asked to list the candidate's greatest strength and worst mistake.

In the interview, candidates were hit with random tough questions such as "How would you design a car for a deaf person?" (The best answer: Plug your ears and drive around to see what it's like to be a deaf driver.) In meetings to discuss the candidates, questions asked ranged from "What do you admire about this candidate?" to "What is he terrible at?"

"One of his mottos was that every time we hired someone, he or she would raise the bar for the next hire, so that the overall talent pool was always improving," said Nicholas Lovejoy, who joined Amazon in 1995 as the fifth employee. Bezos put the philosophy this way: Five years after an employee was hired, he said, that employee should think, "I'm glad I got hired when I did, because I wouldn't get hired now."

However, he managed to get his new employees ridiculously cheap. Amazon was now becoming a hot place to be. Lovejoy already knew Bezos from working with him at D. E. Shaw. He left Shaw to teach math in suburban Seattle for $27,000 per year. Bezos convinced Lovejoy to join his tiny company, but Lovejoy had to take a pay cut.

Bezos also wanted people who did not fit the usual corporate mold. In 1998, Customer Service Director Jane Slade told *Business-Week*, "We tell the temporary recruiting contact agencies, 'Send us your freaks.'" Few of them actually had any prior experience in the bookselling world. But Bezos did lean toward people who had other interests and special talents outside of work—such as people who were champion spellers in grade school, lovers of Baroque music, terrific athletes, or avid mountain climbers. "When you are working very hard and very long hours, you want to be around people who are interesting and fun to be with," Bezos has said. But they also had to be smart. Job candidates were asked to supply their SAT scores and college grade-point averages. One hire was Ryan Sawyer, vice president for strategic growth, a Rhodes Scholar who studied poetry at Oxford.

Bezos kept an unusual work environment. People brought in their dogs, who roamed the new building. That included Jeff and MacKenzie's golden retriever, Kamala, which was named after a metamorph from an episode of *Star Trek: The Next Generation*, titled "The Perfect Mate." Executives held business meetings in the midst of all the chaos. The main office became so crowded that Bezos had to expand into the parking garage on the ground floor. Even the company kitchen served as an office for several people.

Bezos also invested a lot of money to improve the site and add features without making it confusing. He knew that an unhappy customer could spread complaints to thousands of people through Internet chat rooms and newsgroups. From then on, Amazon became an unprofitable business that relentlessly poured its IPO money into new innovations.

These new features also came from many places; the mind of Jeff Bezos, employees, his two-pizza brainstorming teams, even other companies that seemed to have good ideas. They didn't always work out. But often enough, they added real value to the site. These brainstorming sessions, for example, came up with the Gold Box, an animated icon at the top of the page that begged to be clicked on. When that happened, it revealed specials that would last just one hour after customers clicked on it.

Amazon programmer Greg Linden used to tinker with new ideas on his own time. One day he was thinking about the process the company used to automatically check and see if books were available in the warehouse. As soon as someone looked at a book on Amazon, the software would check the inventory list in the background to see if it was in stock so it could tell the customer, if the customer decided to order it. If it was not in stock, the software checked to see how soon the book could be ordered from the distributors, and that meant running off to check the huge databases at the distributors. It was a big piece of software that used up a lot of computer cycles and was very slow. So Linden got an idea. Did the computer really have to check the inventory list every time someone looked at a book? Perhaps the inventory list could be stuck in a cache, essentially put into the memory of the computer running the site, and updated periodically. Then the computer could quickly check the cache without heading off to view the inventory database.

He hacked something together, and found the site could look up the inventory list much more quickly with his idea, although (since the cache was only updated periodically) the data was "a little stale." It was still a prototype, but he started showing it to the other programmers and asking for feedback. It turned out some of them were working on a big redesign of the site, and they wanted to be able to immediately show if a book was available as soon as someone searched on it. So his caching system was "dressed up and pushed out the door." It was a program that no one had asked him to build, but when it showed up, it turned out to be just what the site needed.

One hugely important addition that was critical to Amazon's success was the one Bezos never wanted when he started: huge warehouses from which to distribute books. As Amazon grew, the company could no longer rely on shipments from distributors and publishers to reach customers quickly. It was a miscalculation that Bezos corrected in a big way.

In September 1997, Bezos announced that Amazon would increase its Seattle warehouse by 70 percent and build a new distribution center in New Castle, Delaware. The added warehouse capacity increased the number of books Amazon could hold to 300,000, six times its previous capacity. Although Amazon by this time could tap into a database of 3.1 million books, this new warehouse capacity was enough to stockpile and ship 95 percent of its orders for in-print books the day the orders were received. Amazon could also get these books directly from the publisher instead of from the distribution middlemen. Bezos was now taking the process of stockpiling and distributing books into his own hands. "The logistics of distribution are the iceberg below the waterline of online bookselling," he said at the time.

At the same time, the distributors were trying to build up the top of that iceberg. Ingram decided if it could store and distribute books, it could "drop-ship" them directly to the customers itself. It developed the capability to ship books in small quantities directly to consumers. Then it started opening a few online bookstores to compete with Amazon. The test program failed, however, because its online stores couldn't attract customers. Amazon already had them all. Ingram's next step was to make a bid to buy Barnes & Noble, creating one integrated retailing and distribution conglomerate.

The threat of that combination started a war of press releases. First Bezos issued a release assuring people that he was not intimidated. "Those who make choices that are genuinely good for customers, authors and publishers will prevail. Goliath is always in range of a good slingshot," it read.

—

That shot was not only noticed by the press, but by executives at Barnes & Noble as well. The company issued a response in its own press release: "Barnes & Noble is amused at Jeff Bezos's quote where he describes himself as an independent bookseller. Well, Mr. Bezos, what with market capitalization of some $6 billion, and more than four million customers, we suppose you know a Goliath when you see one. Your company is now worth more than Barnes & Noble, Borders and all of the independent booksellers combined. Might we suggest that slingshots and potshots should not be part of your arsenal."

Of course, that release just served to remind people that Bezos was winning the online bookselling war. So Bezos offered a simple response. He issued another press release that had but one word. "Oh."

Nevertheless, the Ingram and Barnes & Noble deal was never consummated. Independent booksellers also complained, the Federal Trade Commission threatened antitrust action, and Congress got ready to convene its own hearings on the merger. The two companies decided to drop the plan.

Although distributors failed in their attempts to get into Amazon's business, Amazon was able to make inroads into the distributors' business. Bezos knew that shipping most of the books from Amazon's warehouses would be faster. It was a process he could control and improve himself, and the race to build ever larger and more automated distribution centers was on. "There are huge efficiencies to be gained through drop-shipping [from the distributor], but they are paid for by increased complexity in sorting," Bezos said. "Your partner [the distributor] has to be very adept, because if it is done wrong you can really mess up your customer service."

Bezos didn't want to build just any warehouses. His distribution centers had to organize books, find them quickly, match them with shipping orders, package them, and get them in the mail. He wanted the most efficient high-tech distribution centers in the world, and started hiring people to help bring that about. One place he started hiring from was Wal-Mart, known for its computerized distribution centers.

Wal-Mart executives were not pleased. On October 16, 1998, they sued Amazon for hiring away executives who knew trade secrets about its distribution centers, claiming it was an attempt to steal the secrets. The complaint asserted that Amazon was causing it "economic damage." Most of that suit was dismissed, so the following January, it filed a second suit, naming fifteen employees Amazon had taken. It also included Amazon venture capital firm KPCB in the suit, as well as the recently launched online retailer Drugstore.com, of which Amazon owned 46 percent.

Wall Street pundits who follow the companies were perplexed. An online bookseller that would end 1998 with $610 million in revenues and no profit was going to sully the financial picture of a diversified retailing giant that brought in $118 *billion* in revenues? Plus, Wal-Mart's profit, of over $4 billion that year, was nearly seven times Amazon's entire revenue stream. Perhaps Wal-Mart knew something about Amazon's future that most people didn't yet see.

Bezos jumped on the case. To show that he wasn't the only executive who poached key personnel from other companies, he searched Amazon's database for books about Wal-Mart, and purchased three of them. From those he found comments from

Wal-Mart founder Sam Walton about how he liked to troll competitors for new talent. Bezos used that information in Amazon's court filings.

The following April, the companies decided to settle out of court. One former Wal-Mart employee was assigned to a different job at Amazon, and eight others agreed to restrictions in their work assignments with their new employer.

Once he decided to get into the distribution business, Bezos zoomed ahead with his expansion plans. By the end of 1999, he had built five huge high-tech warehouses with computerized systems that tracked the products with bar-code readers and radio transmitters and distributed them to the packing stations along ten miles of conveyor belts. That increased his storage and distribution capability by almost tenfold, to 2.7 million square feet. The company could ship nearly one million boxes a day. "This is the fastest expansion of distribution capacity in peacetime history," he boasted.

He also quadrupled Amazon's computer capacity and increased his staff to five thousand by the end of the year. He had to keep tapping the company's store of publicly traded stock, which kept soaring, in order to finance it all. He took in revenues of $1.5 billion in 1999, but spent over $2 billion.

He had no qualms about spending all that money in order to make sure he could deliver the goods to his customers quickly, easily, and at low cost, even if it meant spending more than he had to. The alternative—trying to just meet demand and taking the risk of having even a few unhappy customers—just wasn't worth it. "You could say we will disappoint some small fraction of people but we will make a lot more money," Bezos said. "But if you disappoint people, you lose brand reputation, and that's worth a lot more to us right now than money."

Besides, the need for all the expanded storage capacity was soon to become clear. He had already decided that Amazon was going to be more than just a bookstore. In December 1996, he had taken executives on a retreat to the Sleeping Lady Resort in Leavenworth, Washington, where they discussed where they would take the company next. The answer, essentially, was, "Everywhere." They even picked out the first likely new markets to pursue: Music CDs, and video and DVD movies. But that was just the beginning. It turned out that the Wal-Mart executives had reason to worry after all.

Chapter 10

Who You Calling a Bookstore?

ezos's plans to expand beyond books started a year before those plans became known to most of the world. By the end of 1998, Bezos had proved his online model was able to compete with physical bookstores, at least in terms of selling, if not in profitability. With sixteen hundred employees at the time, his annual revenues amounted to $375,000 per employee. Barnes & Noble's twenty-seven thousand employees were delivering less than a third of that amount apiece. Since he opened the store in 1995, sales had doubled every 2.4 months, on average. At the end of 1998, sales were still growing at over 300 percent a year, compared to 10 percent at Barnes & Noble. The site was able to turn over its inventory two dozen times a year, compared with three times a year at Barnes & Noble.

Now he was ready to take on more than books. In June of that year, after months of planning, he debuted a music store to sell CDs under the same model he was using to sell books. It had a database of 125,000 titles people could buy, ten times the number most physical music stores had to offer, and the titles were discounted by up to 40 percent. The site included professional and customer reviews, a top-sellers list, music news, recommendations, and an "essentials" list for anyone creating a collection of music. It also offered sound clips of 225,000 songs.

With that announcement, Bezos revealed his true ambition. "Our strategy is to become an electronic commerce destination," he said. "When somebody thinks about buying something online, even if it is something we do not carry, we want them to come to us. We would like to make it easier for people online to find and discover the things they might want to buy online, even if we are not the ones selling them."

Besides, he said, it was something he'd always planned to do, although few people seem to have known it beforehand. In an October interview with the *San Jose Mercury News*, a reporter asked Bezos if selling CDs was a natural outgrowth of Amazon's business or if it was a possibility from the beginning. "We've always said we would expand into areas where we could leverage the three things that businesses can often leverage: our brand name, our skill sets and our customer base," he replied. "Music was a natural place where you can leverage all three of those."

Bezos had help building the site. He could do something no traditional retailer could easily manage. Months before launching, he sent out invitations to "build the music store of your dreams" to Amazon customers. About twenty thousand responded. Although Bezos touted the importance of the feedback, the customers just asked for the same things they liked about Amazon's bookstore: selection, low prices, and convenience. To ensure the last feature, he simply integrated the CD store into Amazon's already existing infrastructure: The site was redesigned to make it easy to switch back and forth between the bookstore and the music store, and features like 1-Click ordering and consolidated shipping worked with both types of products in one shopping basket.

It was not surprising that selling music CDs was the second business he tackled; it was the second choice on the list he had come up with when he first considered starting an online retail business. It was also not surprising, given the rise in Internet commerce, that this time he had to come up against existing competition. CDNow.com and n2k.com had started selling music online at about the same time Amazon started selling books. CDNow had twice the inventory of Amazon's music store. In order to fight off the competition from Amazon, CDNow and n2k decided to merge their companies.

Many observers were as skeptical of Bezos's ability to expand beyond books as they were of his ability to successfully sell books online in the first place. *The Wall Street Journal* called it "risky," saying that "Amazon could lose cachet with bibliophiles if its forays into other media dilute its reputation as a destination for booklovers." Besides, it was going to face competition from bigger companies, such as Columbia House and BMG Entertainment.

One big concern: Getting into new retailing businesses, which have notoriously low margins, might keep the company from ever turning a profit. "The company has been able to show it can sell lots of books for less without making money, and now it has shown it can sell lots of music for less without making money," said Merrill Lynch analyst Jonathan Cohen. Still, most Wall Street analysts were happy that Amazon's soaring stock was making them so much money, and kept their "Buy" ratings, confident that Bezos could keep delivering.

Bezos was equally as confident that he could pull it off. "This is not a winner-take-all kind of business," he said. "On-line commerce is a big arena. It's not going to be the case where you have one company who dominates this marketplace. You are going to have a leader and, clearly, we want to be that leader in every area that we enter into. And the way you become that leader is to focus obsessively on the customer experience. That's why in the book space we're nine times the size of our nearest competitor."

In other words, Bezos felt he simply had to do what he was doing in books: Focus on the consumer and give them what they want. Bezos could leverage all the technology the company had developed for selling books—technology and ease of use its competitors had never managed to match. And he was right. Within four months, Amazon had sold over $14 million worth of CDs, outselling CDNow, the previous leader in selling online music. And, true to the skeptics' assertions, he lost money doing it.

It's important to note that Amazon isn't invincible. Bezos has a simple formula that's not so simple to pull off: Outinnovate the competition and give customers what they want. Companies that have been around long enough to get comfortable forget those mandates. They focus on profits and stock price, believing that raising prices and laying off employees is the way to win. Bezos does not make that mistake.

However, neither is he the world leader in innovation and satisfying customers' needs. Steve Jobs claims that title, and when he put Apple into the business of selling music online by simply offering tunes that could be downloaded electronically, nobody could beat him, including Bezos. It seems that Bezos was focused on physical goods, and neglected to jump in early to offering electronic products for downloading. (After Jobs launched iTunes in April 2003, of course, Bezos caught on to the idea, and started working on the Kindle.)

It didn't take long for Bezos to move beyond CD sales. In November 1997, Bezos made a phone call to Alan Jay, a guy who had created a London-based Web site called the Internet Movie Database (IMDb). The site was a place for movie buffs to post reviews, and to share information about movies, television shows, actors (dead or alive), and trivia. That phone call from an American entrepreneur selling books was a surprise, because the IMDb site didn't sell books, or anything else, for that matter. Originally launched in 1990 and reliant on donations, it didn't even have much of a revenue strategy—it had started accepting advertising and licensing arrangements in 1996.

Bezos proposed a meeting in London. The owners of IMDb met with him for a full day, then had another meeting in Seattle. He offered to invest in the company, promising to keep it free and independent. In April 1998, Amazon bought the entire company, his first acquisition, and set it up as a subsidiary. The reason for the unusual move, of course, was to aid Bezos in his plan to start selling DVD movies online. The acquisition became an advertising venue for Amazon to push DVD sales, which started that November. Forty-five days later, Amazon was the biggest retailer of videos on the Internet. And he still wasn't turning a profit.

In July 1998, Bezos moved beyond selling products with a couple more acquisitions. One was PlanetAll, which offered an Internet-based address book and calendar system. The calendar could also send reminders to email. Many companies offer these services today, but this was a unique offering at the time—and Bezos recognized its significance. "PlanetAll is the most innovative use of the Internet I've ever seen," he said. "It's simply a breakthrough in doing something as fundamental and important as staying in touch. . . . I believe PlanetAll will prove to be one of the most important online applications."

The second was Junglee, a shopping comparison site. When people searched for a product using Junglee, the site would search the Web for other sites selling the product, and list them with the price for each. "Junglee has assembled an extraordinary team of people," Bezos said. "Together we'll empower customers to find and discover the products they want to buy."

With that, Bezos demonstrated that providing a great service for his customers was even more important than making every sale. "We don't even necessarily have to be selling all those things," says Bezos. "We just help people find things that are being sold elsewhere on the Web." It wasn't until Google came along that the idea of actually sending people away from a site was considered a valuable way to gain the goodwill of the public.

But Bezos also had an ulterior motive for these moves. The programs were later incorporated into and replaced by zShops, which later became Amazon Marketplace, where individuals and retailers of all stripes could sell their products through Amazon (which takes a cut from 5 to 25 percent of the sale). That allowed retailers to tap into Amazon's purchasing software and gave buyers confidence that products would arrive as promised.

Most observers—some within Amazon—thought the idea was crazy. Allow competitors to sell through Amazon and compete with products Amazon was also trying to sell? But Bezos knew that people would be able to find other products through the Internet, albeit less easily than finding them on Amazon. By letting them sell through Amazon, he ensured that Amazon remained the best way to find products. And once again conventional wisdom was wrong and Bezos's wisdom was right. Forrester estimates that in the last quarter of 2010, Marketplace accounted for 35 percent of the company's revenues for that quarter.

Not all of Bezos's new retailing ideas worked. In March 1999 he added Amazon Auctions to compete with eBay, and lost. It turned out that eBay was too tough a competitor. But that doesn't detract from his position as a great entrepreneur. The Silicon Valley mantra is to experiment, keep the things that work and drop those that do not. The key is to know when to hold and when to fold.

Also in 1998, Bezos started expanding beyond the United States. His first international sites were in the United Kingdom and Germany. With the Internet taking off, Bezos had decided he once again had to move quickly, especially now that he had money sitting in his public stock just waiting to be tapped. He explained the moves at the time with a sense of urgency, revealing that it was always his intention to expand beyond books:

> Our product extension and geographic expansion is better late than early. Why better late than early? We had to first focus on the book business and grow that until we were comfortable with it. There are always numerous opportunities to expand. We try to err on the side of being slow. Fortunately, we are not capital constrained, but we are definitely people constrained. We only pursue opportunities when the people bandwidth is not constrained. . . . The single most important criterion that we use to acquire a new company is this: Who

are the people behind this venture, and what is the people bandwidth of the acquired company going to be? We are looking for business athletes indoctrinated in this space and companies that have a culture that is common with ours.

When Bezos started moving overseas, German book publishing giant Bertelsmann AG thought a partnership would make sense. Bertelsmann CEO Thomas Middelhoff made an offer. He even sent a corporate jet to fetch Bezos from Turkey, where he was vacationing. Middelhoff's driver went to the airport to pick up the American billionaire when he arrived in Germany, and was surprised to find a casually dressed Bezos toting a bright yellow backpack.

Middelhoff and Bezos met for four hours. Middelhof wanted to create a fifty-fifty joint venture with Amazon in Europe. That deal could have conceivably given Amazon better access to Bertelsmann books, perhaps at a discount, as well as books from other publishing houses the German giant owned, including Random House. Bertelsmann also had a joint venture with America Online in Europe, which could have been another advertising venue for Amazon. Bezos turned the deal down. He didn't say why publicly, simply stating that they couldn't settle on a deal. Middelhoff told the press that he thought Bezos didn't want Bertelsmann to have too much influence. "Jeff was nervous about giving up control," he said.

So Bertelsmann instead offered $300 million for a 50 percent stake in Barnes & Noble's Web site, Barnesandnoble.com. "This venture has one purpose—to compete with Amazon in the U.S.," said Middelhoff.

That deal was like marrying the ugly stepsister, since in the previous six months Barnesandnoble.com had sold just $22 million worth of books, while Amazon had sold nearly ten times that amount. But some observers thought—once again—that the deal could mean trouble for Amazon's expansion plans. Bertelsmann had deep pockets, and all the advantages that could have gone to Amazon would now go to Barnesandnoble.com. *Fortune* magazine asked in a headline, "Is the party over for Amazon?"

Middelhoff put Jonathan Bulkeley, who set up AOL's British operation, in charge of the new venture. *The New York Times* said that Bulkeley's job was "to make Mr. Bezos as miserable as possible." Middelhoff was certain he would succeed. "The future will show who will be better, Jeff or Jonathan," he said. "Personally, I bet on Jonathan."

For his part, Bulkeley talked tough. He noted that Bertelsmann had 4.5 million titles to offer, compared with Amazon's database of 3 million. Barnes & Noble also tried to buy book distributor Ingram, Amazon's biggest supplier of books. "We're motivated. We've got a killer team," noted Bulkeley.

Bulkeley resigned in January 2000, thirteen months after taking on the job. He said he wanted to spend more time with his family and his own investments. The resignation came just after he reported that sales of Barnesandnoble.com had tripled in the previous quarter, to $81.5 million. Amazon's fourth-quarter revenues had increased more than three and a half times, to $250 million. It's not impossible to compete with Amazon, it's just hard to catch its momentum. That fact can be credited to Bezos's determination to get to market first, with the best service, and stay ahead of the competition.

Bezos kept up his mad pace of expansion through 1999, buying or investing in a new company or entering a new business almost every month. He invested in Drugstore.com in February. In March he started the auction business, bought e-Niche (a site for buying and selling music), MusicFind to expand CD sales, Bibliofind for rare books, retailer Accept.com, a company called Alexa Internet, which tracked what sites people visited and recommended others they might find interesting, then added zBubbles to tap Alexa's database in order recommend where to buy products (including those from Amazon) whenever people visited a site reviewing products. That month he also tried to buy Blue Mountain Arts, an online greeting card business, but was rebuffed, so he started his own competitor to Blue Mountain. In May he invested in HomeGrocer.com. In June he invested $45 million in 250-year-old auction house Sotheby's to add high-end items to his auction business. Direct sales of consumer electronics, toys, and games started in July, the same month he bought almost half of sporting goods retailer Gear.com. In September he invested in Della & James, which ran an online wedding gift registry site. He started selling home improvement products, software, video games, and jewelry and leather goods (through a $10 million investment in Ashford.com). He added a Gift Ideas feature in November and signed an agreement with Next-Card, Inc., in order to offer an Amazon-branded Visa card. That was also the month he announced zShops, the precursor of Amazon Marketplace, to let businesses and individuals sell products through Amazon.

With that last announcement, he also changed Amazon's logo. Instead of a logo in which the letter A in Amazon was designed to look like a flowing river, it became simply the word *Amazon*, with a swooping arrow underneath to point from the letter A to the letter Z in the name. The idea was that consumers could now use Amazon to buy any product, from A to Z, even if Amazon didn't sell the product itself. And if it did sell a product but someone else had it cheaper, Bezos would let customers buy it from the lower-priced retailer through Amazon.

He explained it at the time as an almost altruistic feature for customers. "In the categories where we are selling things directly, if we can't be competitive then we shouldn't be standing in the way of our customers," he said at the zShops announcement. However, he also made it clear that he wouldn't stand in the way of his customers as long as they didn't try to leave the Amazon store. "We really don't care whether we sell something through zShops, or sell something directly ourselves; it is sort of a wash for us," he added. "You can't sell everything on your own. You need to band together with third parties."

But the big message was this: No matter what anyone wanted to buy, they could probably get the best price by going through Amazon. If it wasn't the absolute best price, the difference was probably worth the security one got with an Amazon transaction. It's a reputation that Amazon still holds today.

There was, however, one bit of negative backlash to Amazon's incredible dominance. With the purchase of Alexa and Amazon's ability to recommend products that it knew its customers might like, people began to realize that the online retailing giant was collecting an astounding amount of information about their buying habits and interests. That made some people feel just a bit queasy. In January 2000, a San Francisco man filed a lawsuit complaining that Alexa was sending his personal information to Amazon without his permission. At the same time, Internet security consultant

Richard M. Smith filed a complaint with the Federal Trade Commission saying that Amazon collected more personal info than it let on.

Amazon had to start disclosing its practices more openly in privacy statements that nobody ever read in order to quell the rising controversy. In fact, Amazon is still one of the most impressive machines for collecting data about people who use its services. These days, however, Google has displaced Amazon as the anti-privacy bogeyman. (When Google announced its bookselling business in 2010, privacy advocates even complained that would give the company too much information about what books people are buying, seemingly having forgotten about Amazon's database altogether.)

Still, throughout 1999, Amazon's stock price continued to soar like Icarus trying out new wings. Wall Street analysts and others who kept warning about the company's lack of profitability were dismissed as old economy pessimists who didn't understand the new economy of the Internet. In April 1998, Keith Benjamin, an Internet analyst with BancAmerica Robertson Stephens in San Francisco, enthusiastically called Amazon "the poster child of Internet commerce." Amazon was also the poster child for Henry Blodget, an Internet analyst with Merrill Lynch, who became famous for his seemingly uncanny projections of the amazing growth of Amazon and other Internet stocks.

But the number of skeptics was also growing. There were plenty of knowledgeable people who believed the Internet economy was a bubble that had to pop someday. The question was when it would happen. But when it did happen, they felt, Amazon would be vulnerable. In 1999, the company reported a loss of $720 million, and had amassed $2 billion in debt, which was costing the company $125 million a year in interest. How could Amazon continue without the ever-soaring stock price, which provided Bezos with cash and equity to build warehouses, add inventory, and buy more companies in his grandiose dream to create the greatest retailing firm on earth?

A commentary article in a March 1999 edition of *The New York Times* by book author Peter de Jonge summed up the skepticism: "For all its all-nighters and tattooed punks humping books in the distribution center and golden retrievers wandering the halls in the corporate office," De Jonge wrote, "Amazon.com is a $20 billion, 2,100-employee company built on the thin membrane of a bubble, and this brings a manic precariousness to the place that no amount of profitless growth can diminish." In November 1999, *Barron's* magazine named Amazon (along with Microsoft) the most overvalued stock on the market.

Nobody really knew which view was right. But by the end of 1999, everyone was sure of one thing: Jeff Bezos had forever transformed the business of retailing. He claimed that Amazon now sold eighteen million different items through its site. In December 1999, Bezos was named *Time* magazine's "Person of the Year." Bezos had reached the pinnacle of an industry he had created, and it seemed like nobody could touch him. By that time, the mountain that he lorded over like Moses on the Mount had already started crumbling beneath his feet. The only milestone he hadn't accomplished yet was the one he claimed wasn't important: He still hadn't turned a profit.

Chapter 11

The Crash

In June 1999, Black & Decker executive Joseph Galli accepted an offer to become president and CEO of PepsiCo's Frito-Lay North America Division. Then Bezos got to him. In a long meeting, Bezos convinced him to kiss off Frito-Lay and join him atop Amazon's summit as president and chief operating officer. After the purchase of mail-order tool-seller Tool Crib of the North, Galli helped Amazon get into the business of selling tools online, a much higher-margin business than the others Amazon had entered recently. Contractors could order tools on Amazon and have them shipped directly to their job sites.

That was the fun part of the job. The following January, Bezos, at least, said he was still having a great time. "I'm just plain having fun at Amazon.com," he said. "I'm a change junkie, and I can't imagine an environment more changing than the Internet in general and Amazon.com in particular."

Well, the Internet was changing, all right. After the Y2K scare turned out to be less threatening than a two-year-old's Halloween costume, everybody stopped upgrading the computers they had previously feared would crash, sending airplanes plummeting from the sky. Instead, sales of computers and other tech products did the plummeting, starting January 1, 2000. Within a few months, as the terrible sales started showing up in quarterly financial reports, tech stocks followed suit, and the dot-com bubble imploded like stars into a black hole.

Amazon's crash coincided with the dot-com crash, which became apparent after Amazon reported its first quarter results in April 2000 (the first quarter after Y2K-induced buying stopped). The crash certainly contributed to the collapse of Amazon's stock price. But it does not account for the sudden slowing in Amazon's revenues. After all, most of Amazon's revenues came from non-tech products, so the end of the tech-buying binge should not have hurt Amazon as much as other tech companies.

But signs of trouble at Amazon began even before Y2K hit and ran. Even as late as December 1999, analysts were projecting a net loss for Amazon of as much as $350 million. But the loss came in at a whopping $720 million, even though revenues had more than doubled, to $1.6 billion.

The year 2000 merely exacerbated the problems that had started at Amazon in the year Y1.999K. After years of annual reports to shareholders that began with a letter full of hyperactive hyperbole about the previous spectacular year, Bezos began his letter for the year 2000 annual report with: "Ouch. It's been a brutal year for many in the capital markets and certainly for Amazon.com shareholders." After years of triple-digit growth, revenues in 2000 grew just 68 percent, to $2.8 billion. Further, Amazon reported a $1.4 billion loss, compared to a $654 million loss the year before.

For almost any other multibillion-dollar company in the world,

68 percent growth would have been spectacular. But Amazon had grown too big in too short a time. Bezos's strategy of growing as fast as possible worked, putting the company into a position that made it almost impossible for anyone to catch (even today), at least in retailing. But the company had also started to spin out of control, plagued by inefficiency and overcapacity. With everything in high gear and the gas pedal to the floor, it was not able to stop quickly enough to avoid slamming into the wall that suddenly appeared around the Y2K bend.

At the end of 1999, for example, Amazon's most recent warehouse, an 850,000-square-foot behemoth in Coffeyville, Kansas, was only 10 percent utilized. Bezos was anticipating that the company's continued torrid growth into new markets would fill the warehouse with new products soon enough. He was still pursuing the strategy that it was better to have too much capacity now than not enough when needed, which would delay the delivery of products and anger customers. As Bezos had once quipped, like the joke about obstetricians, "One baby dropped on its head is too many."

His ambition truly had no bounds, his head full of new ideas on what to add next. By mid-1999, he was talking about Amazon getting into travel services, banking, insurance, and other businesses far afield from retailing. And what if other Web sites came along to offer even lower prices than Amazon? "Membership clubs!" he said in December. "If you want to see all the information we collect on Amazon—the customer reviews, the professional reviews and use our agenting technology—you have to pay $30 a year."

But at the same time, increased competition was also taking its toll, despite Amazon's rapid growth and domination of new markets. In fact, Bezos apparently knew that trouble lay ahead as early as the summer of 1999. Revenues were more than doubling, but losses were also growing in step with his ambitions.

That started worrying more Wall Street stock analysts, who had been blown away with Amazon's growth and stock trajectory until then. When Amazon held its quarterly conference call with analysts in June 1999, the Street was less impressed than usual. "Everyone thinks [the problems] all happened in April of this year [2000]," recalled Kelyn Brannon, Amazon's former CFO, in a December 2000 story in *Fortune* magazine. "We saw the turn—how the market was going—after the June [1999] conference call. The tone of the calls, the questions, the whisper conversations that went on afterward—it was a different tone. Rather than saying great quarter, great revenue growth—we stopped getting so many 'greats.' You get right into hard questions: Can you talk to me about direct margin? Can you talk to me about the operational efficiencies in your distribution center?" Brannon left Amazon six months after that conference call.

Galli was the one who had to straighten things out. In January 2000, he had to play the heavy and lay off 150 people in order to start putting Amazon on a path toward profitability. He hired new managers who knew how to run a company more efficiently, implemented tighter budgets, requiring all major purchases to be approved by top management. He became the symbol of Amazon's transformation from a very cool new-age Internet company to a more buttoned-down corporation that was actually prone to recession like every other company in the world. He even took away the employees' free aspirin and Tylenol—a move that created such an outcry that he had to restore it a week later. Employees were getting a lot of headaches.

As the recession deepened in 2000 and Amazon's stock plummeted like spit off a bridge, Galli himself began to need some of that Tylenol. In July 2000, a little more than a year after he had joined Amazon, the company announced that he was leaving. He took over as president and CEO of VerticalNet, an Internet company that ran dozens of industry-specific Web sites. Galli and Bezos insisted that things were fine between them, and that Galli decided to change jobs to get closer to his children, who lived with his former wife in Baltimore. VerticalNet was in Horsham, Pennsylvania. But VerticalNet was (and is) no Amazon. It never recovered from the Y2K fiasco, and in 2007 was sold to an Italian cement company.

Wall Street wondered if there was more to Galli's departure than family needs. For one thing, the previous CEO of VerticalNet said that he hadn't even been looking for a new CEO, that Galli had approached him about the job. And the timing of Galli's departure was odd: He quit the day before Amazon announced its second-quarter earnings. "Well, it's never a good sign when your president resigns a day before earnings," said Mark Rowen, a market analyst at Prudential Securities, the day Galli resigned. He suspected trouble. "The truth is, nothing goes from a small business to an extremely large business without any hiccups," Rowen said. "And I think we're seeing a hiccup at Amazon."

What Amazon suffered was more of a seizure than a hiccup. It's just that most Wall Street analysts were hoping Bezos would still pull Amazon out of its revenue spasm. But when he announced that Amazon had taken in just $578 million in sales for the quarter, $22 million less than some Wall Street analysts had hoped for, six analysts immediately downgraded the stock. Because of cost-cutting measures, Amazon's net loss was less than Wall Street had expected, but stockholders were hoping that increasing revenues would help it generate a profit that year. The stock dropped 13 percent that day. In total, thirteen analysts downgraded Amazon's rating in the year 2000. Between mid-December 1999 and the end of 2000, Amazon's stock lost 90 percent of its value, bottoming out at about $15 per share.

Was Amazon now toast? People had finally given up on unprofitable Internet companies, and Amazon was the biggest money-loser on the Internet. In the previous five years, Bezos had borrowed $2 billion—and had lost $1.74 billion of it. Wall Street started calling on Bezos to grow up and start running the company like a business, not a gambling casino. "It's time for these guys to start performing like real retailers," said Gene Alvarez, a retail analyst at research firm Meta Group. "The Internet panache has worn off and now it's time to start performing."

Bezos took the criticism to heart. He complained that he had gone from "Internet poster child to Internet whipping boy." At the same time, he finally changed the tune he had been singing—or perhaps whistling in the dark—for years. "Get Big Fast" was dead. He was now going to work on turning a profit.

To be fair, this shift was, in a sense, all part of his plan. During a Q&A session with employees at a spanking-new distribution center in December 1999, he said he would switch to a strategy of working toward a profit when the "cone of opportunity" on the Internet had sufficiently narrowed to make it difficult for newcomers to squeeze through ahead of him, to gain a foothold in all the new markets he was contemplating. Bezos just didn't realize that the cone would suddenly close altogether.

Once that happened, though, Bezos adopted his new religion with all the fervor he had previously used to worship the god of growth. A December 2000 article in *Fortune* magazine noted that he mentioned the word *profit* twenty-five times in an interview with the magazine. One of the mentions: "We have, for the first time, set an internal goal with the date for when the company as a whole is going to be profitable," he declared.

Bezos even showed the *Fortune* reporter an email he had circulated to the company's seven thousand employees to prove it. It read: "We're putting a stake in the ground: We're going to become profitable. That's right: We're aiming to have sales of $5 billion, produce over $1 billion in gross profits, and achieve solid operating profitability by . . ." (Bezos had blotted out the date, since he had a policy against making forward-looking statements. But the reporter got the date from another Amazon employee: Christmas 2001.)

Bezos did what any stockholder-fearing CEO would do: He slashed costs by laying people off and cutting spending. His inspirational posters preaching about growth were replaced with something more down-to-earth: "Get the CRAP [Can't Realize Any Profit] Out." He also started running Amazon more like a retailer than like a dot-com company, with both eyes on the bottom line. He closed unprofitable lines of business, wrote off bad investments, increased cost-cutting, and started demanding more realistic budgets. Every division head had to meet with him weekly to go over the division's budget. Each executive had to submit budgets with specific revenue goals, and timelines by which they would be met. Amazon managers started taking Finance 101 courses at the company's Seattle headquarters.

Bezos also tried to reassure Wall Street that he was cracking the cost-cutting whip at managers. At the third-quarter conference call with stock analysts, he said he had been telling managers that "we want you to find half a million dollars, we want you to find $750,000, we want you to find $1.5 million." Those reassurances failed to inspire confidence. After the meeting, Amazon's stock price dropped 17 percent. People hadn't heard this kind of backtracking from the always gung-ho Bezos before.

That didn't mean, however, that he put the brakes on Amazon's expansion into new retail products. In 2000, he added sales of lawn and patio furniture, health and beauty aids, and kitchen products to the mix. He also made investments in living.com, Audible.com, and online car-sales company Greenlight.com. These companies, however, also paid Amazon hefty fees to be featured on Amazon's Web site, still prime virtual property on the Internet. Bezos's ambitions had not abated one bit. "The question now becomes, how much of the $5 trillion worldwide [retail] market is addressable?" Bezos said during the Wall Street conference call.

In October 2000, Amazon started showing improvement, this time giving Wall Street a pleasant surprise. Its quarterly loss came in at 25 cents a share. Most analysts had been expecting a loss of about 33 cents a share. There were other good signs: Operating losses were 11 percent of revenues, half what they had been a year earlier, while gross profit margins were up to 26 percent, compared to 20 percent a year earlier. Bezos had finally learned the trick most public companies had lived by for years: Never surprise

Wall Street unless it's with good news. The stock regained about 30 percent of its value over the next three days.

It wasn't the end of Amazon's troubles, though. The company still struggled with a tough market throughout 2001, and its stock again receded. In early 2001, he laid off another thirteen hundred employees, about 15 percent of the workforce, including customer service workers, closing down a service center in Seattle. He also shuttered a warehouse in Georgia.

During this time he started another business that brought in immediate revenues: building and running Web sites for other companies, including Toys "R" Us, Target, Circuit City, and even book retailer Borders.

But those deals were done, in part, to make up for declines in Amazon's core business. In the third quarter of 2000, for example, Amazon sold $400 million worth of books, music, and videos. A year later that had dropped to $351 million. One analyst estimated that quarterly revenue per customer had dropped from $31 per employee to just $18 per customer in late 2001.

The Toys "R" Us deal, announced in August 2000, was a particularly big shift in strategy for Amazon. The deal was set to last ten years, during which Amazon would help the toy retailer rebuild and run its site, Toysrus.com. The toy company hadn't done a particularly good job on its own, suffering through many site crashes and late deliveries. Amazon would handle the purchases, shipping, and customer service, but Toys "R" Us would own the inventory, which meant Bezos didn't have to spend money buying products up front. Toys "R" Us took the risk of paying for the inventory—including buying Amazon's toy inventory—while Amazon would stock all the toys sold online in its underused warehouses. That made things much easier for Amazon, since toys usually had to be ordered from Asian manufacturers six months in advance. Bezos didn't want to be in the position of having to write off more unsold inventory. This deal was the start of Amazon's business of selling products from other retailers through its site.

The deal, however, didn't last ten years. While it was hailed as a good deal for both companies at the time, getting them both out of the problems they were facing in online toy sales, both companies wanted out once their problems were behind them. In 2003, Amazon started allowing other toy retailers to sell through its site. In 2004, Toys "R" Us sued for $200 million in damages and the right to get out of the deal, saying that Amazon had agreed to sell only its toys through Amazon.com. Bezos countersued, asserting that the toy retailer had failed to provide Amazon with enough inventory to meet demand. In 2007, a court ruled that Toys "R" Us could terminate the agreement, but awarded no damages. The previous year, electronics retailer Circuit City ended a similar relationship with Amazon after four years.

But in 2001, Bezos had his eye on a much closer horizon. At the fall earnings conference call, he said he expected to start making a profit by the end of the year. He was, however, very specific, promising only a pro forma net profit (a profit before most expenses are taken into account). He kept cutting back in the fourth quarter, reducing operating costs by half. That allowed him to further lower prices on books, music, and videos, with the hope that people would buy more.

It worked. On January 22, 2002, he made the conference call with analysts to reveal the results of the fourth quarter of 2001. Not only had he made the pro forma net, he reported the company's first net profit after all expenses were taken out. It wasn't much: just $5 million, or a penny a share. But it was much nicer than the $545 million net loss he'd reported a year earlier. This was to become a key contributor to Amazon's future profitability. By running the company more efficiently, he could keep prices as low as possible, cementing Amazon's reputation as the go-to place for online retail.

Try as he might, he could barely contain his enthusiasm. "As pleased as we are with this quarter, we have a ton of work to do," Bezos said during the conference call. Still, listeners could hear Amazon executives applauding and slapping high fives with each other at the end of the call.

They had reason to be happy. In four days, the stock rose 42 percent. That was still only a price of $14.44, but a huge gain for anyone who bought Amazon near the bottom.

And now that he had proved, at last, that he could run a profitable business, he continued Amazon's expansion, albeit at a less frenetic pace. In June 2002, he opened for business in Canada. In September he started selling office products. In November he started selling apparel. But his most important new business would not arrive until 2007. It was a new piece of hardware developed just for Amazon, called the Kindle.

Chapter 12

Bezos Bets Big on the Kindle

The CEO of the largest bookstore on earth believes that books have had "a great five hundred year run." But now, he insists, "it's time to change."

Some people may still love the musty smell of old books, the crispness of print on paper pages, or the comfort of a solid book like an old friend. Bezos disagrees. He's ready to toss them into the recycling bin to make way for new technology. "I'm grumpy when I'm forced to read a physical book because it's not as convenient," he complains. "Turning the pages . . . the book is always flopping itself shut at the wrong moment."

Bezos insists—and others agree—that the Kindle is simply a better form of book. Once again, he resorted to the strategy he first used when starting an online store: making the product something unique rather than simply imitating the physical version. "You can't ever outbook the book," Bezos said, "so you have to do things that you can't do with a book, such as in-stream dictionary lookup, changing fonts, and wireless delivery of content in 60 seconds. We have to build something better than a physical book."

That Bezos would so readily reject the paper product that started his company should not be a big surprise. He's an electronics guy, a fan of products written in base two computer code: 00 01 10 11 100 101 ... It's the final content that's important, whether delivered with type on a page or with bits shot through cyberspace to an electronic reader. And manufacturing and delivering electronic books is much, much cheaper than manufacturing and delivering the paper kind.

But it took another brilliant entrepreneur to give him the idea. Except for Web services, Bezos sold only physical goods in Amazon's first decade. Then, on March 4, 2003, Apple's Steve Jobs demonstrated that some physical products were unnecessary. The music CD was simply a way of delivering the real product, the music itself. But music can be digitized and shipped over the Internet without the cost of the physical CD or the expense of mailing. The iTunes music store was born.

Sometime in 2004 Bezos had an Amazon executive approach Gregg Zehr, a hardware developer who had worked at Apple and at palmOne, which created the Palm personal digital assistant. The executive asked Zehr to start a new company in order to create a new electronic book reader for Amazon. Zehr reportedly asked why he should be interested. The answer: "To change the world."

The start-up, called, mysteriously, Lab126, was kept very quiet for years. It is located in Cupertino, in the Silicon Valley, where Zehr recruited other developers from Apple and Palm. Lab126 would only reveal on its Web site that it was working on a "groundbreaking, highly integrated consumer product." One blogger who only identified himself as "j" came across the company's Web site in early 2006 and speculated that Lab126 was creating a competitor to Apple's iPod, or perhaps a smart phone. The mystery was solved on November 19, 2007, when Bezos announced the first Kindle e-book reader.

But is Bezos really that tired of physical books? One can never tell when his hyperbole is real or when he's just trying to sell a product. In October 2005, for example, even as Lab126 was getting started on the Kindle, he introduced a new feature that would allow customers to access pages of a book electronically through the Web site for a few cents a page. Or, for $1.99 per book, they could read as many pages of a book as they wished through their computer. At that time, he insisted that reading electronic books and paper books were separate products. "For the kind of book where you have long reading sessions, you will still want the physical book, but there may be times when you want to access [short sections of] a book for reference purposes," he said at the time. Or, he suggested, impatient customers waiting for the book they just ordered to arrive from Amazon may spend two bucks to get started immediately. One likely scenario is that he was testing the idea of paying for access to digital books while the Kindle was being tested.

Amazon was not the first company to offer electronic books. In fact, people had been toying with the idea for decades before the Kindle arrived. In 1968, Alan Kay, then at Xerox Corporation's Palo Alto Research Center, conceived of the Dynabook, a graphics-based portable computer (a concept which Steve Jobs later borrowed to create the Macintosh). But Kay also saw the device as an e-book, a way to download and carry around digitized books.

That meant people would have to have access to digitized books. So in 1971, Michael Hart, a student at the University of

Illinois, Champaign-Urbana (where the Mosaic Web browser was later invented), started Project Gutenberg, the first project to digitize and archive written works, mostly books in the public domain. The project now has some thirty-five thousand works in its archive. The effort was an attempt "to encourage the creation and distribution of eBooks."

In the 1990s, companies started offering e-book devices in earnest. A company called Digital Book, Inc., sold floppy disks containing fifty digitized books in 1993. Within a few years, now-forgotten e-book readers such as Cybook, RocketBook, and SoftBook were reaching the market. Most sold in the range of $300 to $500, although one, the Everybook—which had twin facing color screens so that it could open like a real book—sold for $1,600. Online retailers started offering books in electronic form for sale in 1999. Even Microsoft got into the game by announcing a software program called Microsoft Reader, designed specifically to read electronic books, in 2000. They were all commercial failures.

Still, the field kept progressing. Random House and Harper-Collins started digitizing some of their books in 2002. Google started digitizing public-domain books in 2004. Sony Corporation launched its first e-book in 2006. A year later, the Sony Reader was widely considered a dud, which Sony denied, although the company refused to reveal any sales numbers.

By 2006, people were beginning to question whether the public even wanted digital books, even as Apple's iPod popularized the business of downloading digital music through the Internet and directly into a portable device. "Consumers have proven time and again that they would prefer to buy and keep physical books," Evan

Wilson, an analyst with Pacific Crest Securities who covers Sony, told *BusinessWeek* magazine in September 2007.

In early 2007, the rumors began to circulate about Amazon's coming e-book reader. Sony tried to turn up the heat in August by adding software from Adobe that would allow its Reader to download electronic books from other sources. It dropped the price by $50, to $250. It took out ads in publications such as *The New York Times*, *USA Today*, and *Vanity Fair*. It offered first-time buyers credits for one hundred free classic titles. Those tactics didn't work either.

Then, on November 19, 2007, Bezos stood before a crowd of reporters at the W Union Square Hotel in Manhattan to announce the Kindle, an electronic book-reading device that he would sell for $399. Bezos has never said how many of the devices were available when the Kindle was first announced, but he did make a point of saying that they sold out in five and a half hours. It remained on back order for months. The online magazine *TechCrunch* cited a source claiming that by July 2008 Amazon had sold 240,000 of the devices. The book publishing industry was irrevocably changed.

The early versions of e-books, it turned out, simply had too many flaws. Some people didn't like the design of the products. The Sony Reader was criticized as having a confusing interface with too many buttons. In order to download books, it had to be connected to a computer. But the big problem was a severe lack of the most important aspect of an e-book reader: the electronic books themselves. Sony's product, for example, could only pull books from Sony's online service called Connect, which had just about one-tenth the number of titles available at a good-sized bookstore.

Bezos overcame those flaws with his usual approach: attention to detail. The Kindle is simple to use. It includes wi-fi, allowing it to connect directly to Amazon without going through a separate computer. Once an electronic book is purchased from Amazon, it downloads seamlessly within seconds into the Kindle (and, more recently, other devices the buyer designates, such as the iPad, iPod, iPhone, and Android phones). Simply click or tap on the title of the book on the screen and the e-book opens to the last page you've read. It leverages the technology of electronics and the Internet to do things paper books cannot, such as allowing customers to tap on a word to call up its definition.

One of the important issues that Lab126 dealt with was the complaint that reading text on a computer screen for long periods tires the eyes. So Lab126 incorporated into the Kindle technologies called "electronic paper" and "electronic ink." First developed in the 1970s at Xerox Corporation's Palo Alto Research Center (PARC), it mimics the look of ink on paper by using electrically charged particles, black on one side and white on the other, which could be selectively flipped over with electrical charges to create black letters on a white screen. The Kindle—like Sony's earlier e-book—used technology from a company called E Ink Corporation. Founded in 1997 as a spin-off of the Media Lab at the Massachusetts Institute of Technology, it developed a slightly different approach using charged particles.

The e-ink display contains millions of "microcapsules," each one filled with white particles with a positive charge and black particles with a negative charge. The microcapsules are sandwiched between two layers of electrodes. Most of the screen keeps a negative charge on the top layer of electrodes and a positive charge on the bottom, pulling the white particles to the top of the microcapsules and the black to the bottom. That creates a white background on the screen. In order to form letters, the polarity of the electrodes is reversed in specific spots, pulling the black capsules to the top and forming black letters. Since the page is formed with particles, and not electrons, it looks like particles of ink on a page. And the particles don't dance like electrons being constantly refreshed. Once the page is formed, the particles remain in place without applying more power to it, saving battery life and creating stable, unblinking letters. All it needs is a quick flash of power to form the next page.

Sony had many of the same features, but not as well implemented. Its first readers apparently used e-ink technology that wasn't yet ready for the best-seller list. When a page was erased and a new one created, it produced an annoying flash between pages. The technology from Lab126 didn't have the same problem.

Bezos also had a big advantage: With access to virtually every publisher in the world, he could offer ninety thousand e-books when the Kindle was first released in 2007. The original device could store two hundred books at once.

Despite its technology and Bezos's claims of quick sales, the press was as skeptical of the Kindle's potential as they were of Amazon's ability to fend off competition a decade earlier. The Kindle was ugly. (*TechCrunch* accurately described it as something that "looks like it came out of the 70's.") At $400, it was too expensive, as was the price of $10 per book. And it seemed as though it would be difficult to make the e-ink technology cheap enough to bring down the price significantly. "E Ink's technology isn't enough to make Kindle the breakthrough e-reading device that I and thousands of other e-book fans have been waiting for," wrote the respected technology journalist Wade Roush on the technology site Xconomy.

These days, Bezos is on a zealous campaign to popularize his Kindle e-book reader device and relegate the paper book to the dusty shelves of library archives. He has repeatedly said that the Kindle is the best-selling product on Amazon. But his definition of "product" is obscure. It's difficult to believe, for example, that Amazon sells more Kindles than it does the e-books to read on them, or even paper-based books. In terms of revenues, however, the Kindle may be a bigger product, since one Kindle costs $200 to $500, while the electronic books are usually $10 to $14 apiece.

But the Kindle has unquestionably had an impact. Since it was released the question among publishers has gone from "Do people really want electronic books?" to "Do people want to read physical books anymore?" Jeff Bezos single-handedly turned publishing upside down with the Kindle. By December 2010, e-books were accounting for up to 10 percent of the revenues at some large publishers, despite the fact that the publishers sell e-books at half the price of hardcover books. That implies that just after three years on the market, up to 20 percent of books at some publishers are sold in electronic form.

Bezos is so avid about e-books, in fact, that he has been willing to sell them at a loss. In order to keep his cut-rate $9.99 price for most e-books, Bezos is reselling them at a loss of up to five dollars for each discounted book he sells. Bezos clearly sees it as the future of the business that got Amazon started, and is determined to remain the leader in this category by keeping competitors from getting a foothold on the virtual bookshelf.

But it's getting harder for him to maintain his pricing strategy. Bezos has tried to use muscle against publishers to force them to sell electronic books to him more cheaply, just as he has done with paper versions. Publishers fear that customers will become accustomed to cheap e-books (a fear that might already have some truth behind it), forcing them to put a wholesale price on e-books that will not allow the publishers to make a profit. So they are switching to a new pricing structure for e-books. In the new "agency model," publishers are demanding that they set the retail price of the e-books, generally $12.99 to $14.99, just as they do for the paper versions. The publishers will keep 70 percent of the price to themselves. The retailers can then offer discounts if they want, but they have to take it out of their 30 percent.

Bezos does not like this scenario and has been doing everything he can to stop it. On January 28, 2010, Macmillan CEO John Sargent traveled to Seattle to give Amazon his proposal for the agency model. If Amazon did not accept it, Sargent told the executives that they could keep their old model, but that would result in (as he wrote in his blog) "extensive and deep winnowing of titles" available to Amazon. Within a week, Amazon had removed all Macmillan books—paper and electronic—from its site, except those sold through Amazon by third parties.

The tactic failed. Bezos had to give in to Sargent's demands and within another week had restored Macmillan's books to the site. This was, no doubt, due partly to the fact that Steve Jobs had already agreed to the agency model, which could have given Apple better access to e-books from placated publishers. On the other hand, in October 2010 Amazon offered to pay royalties of 70 percent to authors who self-publish through the Kindle store, compared to 25 percent from most publishers.

For now, the Kindle still leads the market for e-book readers at its current price. Research company ChangeWave estimated that the Kindle had the largest share of the market in early 2011, at 47 percent. Apple's iPad (which does much more than just read books and is more expensive) had a 32 percent share. The Sony Reader and the Barnes & Noble Nook were laggards, with just 5 percent and 4 percent of the market, respectively.

But the Kindle may not hold its lead forever. Before Apple's iPad was released, Amazon practically owned the e-book reader market. And other competitors keep trying. Barnes & Noble has come out with a color version of the Nook, to compete with the black-and-white Kindle. At the end of 2010 Barnes & Noble echoed earlier statements from Bezos when it announced that the Nook Color has become the best-selling item it has ever sold. Aside from its own stores, Barnes & Noble also sells the Nook through other retailers such as Best Buy and Wal-Mart. The company said it sold more than a million e-books on Christmas day 2010.

And Google is making it tough for Bezos to strong-arm publishers for heavy discounts on e-books. In December 2010, it launched its own online store, called Google eBooks, to sell all those books it has been digitizing itself. Google is supplying applications to allow people to buy and download its e-books to every appropriate device, from the iPad to smart phones, except one: the Kindle. That could either limit Google's market (if the Kindle remains popular) or force Amazon to open the Kindle to e-books sold by other vendors (the format Kindle uses makes that difficult today).

Publishers, once resistant to Google's book-digitizing project, are now embracing Google's efforts, since Google has agreed to the agency model. Even brick-and-mortar stores love Google's approach, because they can now start selling e-books themselves. Google is allowing independent bookstores to sell its e-books through their own Web sites.

Retailers are confident, at least for now, that Google will not try to take the whole market for itself. "Google's business model is not to be a retailer," says Oren Teicher, CEO of the American Booksellers Association. He believes Google will allow independent bookstores to more effectively compete against Amazon. "The fact that the cost of technology has come way down means that you don't need to be an international monolith to use technology," he says. The bookstores, be believes, will do a better job of recommending new books to their online customers, just as they do their store customers. "We're good at putting the right book in buyers' hands. We have knowledge and passion about books."

Bezos, on the other hand, has a passion about electronic business models. He's sure to keep advancing the Kindle in order to stay at the top of the market. His strategy has been to focus on a dedicated e-book reader, not a general-purpose device. That allows him to use technologies such as electronic ink, which refreshes too slowly for computers—it takes about as long for the next page to appear as it does to turn the page of a paper book—but is better for long-term reading and is still legible in bright sunlight. It's not certain, however, if that tactic will last. With new competitors racing into the market like an invading army, his early lead in the market might not sustain its momentum.

There's definitely a huge future market in e-books. Market researcher Forrester estimates that people bought $1 billion worth of e-books in 2010, and that by 2015 that will grow to $3 billion annually. The question is whether Amazon should focus on the Kindle or the e-books themselves. Rather than discounting the e-books, one argument says, Bezos may be considering eventually making the Kindle free. He has already dropped one version to $139—cheaper, as his TV ads say, than a good pair of designer sunglasses. In October 2009, blogger John Walkenbach graphed the declining price of the Kindle, and noticed it was on a straight-line trajectory that pointed to zero in the second half of 2011. Author and blogger Kevin Kelly asked Bezos about that trend line in August 2010. Bezos smiled and said, "Oh, you noticed that." And then smiled again.

Then Michael Arrington at *TechCrunch* came up with a business model that would make it possible. In January 2010, Amazon made a great offer to select customers: Buy a Kindle, but if you don't like it, get a full refund—and keep the device. Arrington believes that it was a test run to see what the economic outcome of a free Kindle would turn out to be. He quotes "a reliable source" that says Bezos wants to give a free Kindle to every Amazon Prime subscriber, Amazon customers who pay $79 a year to get unlimited free two-day shipping and one-day shipping for $3.99 per item.

Amazon Prime subscribers are the company's best customers, those most likely to buy a lot of e-books from Amazon, covering the cost of giving away a free reader.

For now, Bezos isn't talking, but he clearly sees e-books as a huge part of Amazon's future. Market researchers estimate that

Amazon sells three out of every four e-books sold. The question is whether the Kindle itself will be a part of that future. After all, Amazon also provides free applications that allow people to turn their computers and cell phones into e-readers in order to buy and download e-books from Amazon. People can even get free e-books—classics no longer under copyright—from Amazon's store. Besides, although the Kindle is one of the most important products Bezos has introduced in years, it isn't the only one. Although he hasn't started offering insurance policies through Amazon.com (yet), he has been figuring out new ways to make money without selling physical products. His ambition still knows no bounds.

Chapter 13

———

Is Amazon Killing the Bookstore?

Amazon.com is not going to put bookstores out of business.
Barnes & Noble is opening a new superstore every four days.
Borders is opening a new superstore every nine days.

—Jeff Bezos in 1998

Barnes & Noble is no longer opening a couple of new stores nearly every week. It has recently spent its time closing them. In early 2010 the world's biggest bookstore chain shut down the last of its B. Dalton bookstores, which it acquired in 1986 and once boasted eight hundred stores. Barnes & Noble racked up $107 million in losses in the first nine months of its fiscal year in 2010.

Borders Group, Inc., the second largest bookstore chain, is suffering like a CEO with swine flu. It has lost a total of $605 million over the last four years. The company announced on December 30, 2010, that it would delay payments to some publishers while it tries to refinance its debt.

———

In order to remain competitive, the second-largest shareholder of Borders stock, William Ackman of Pershing Square Capital Management, has proposed an unusual tactic: buying Barnes & Noble, a company more than twice its size. In December 2010, Ackman proposed a price of nearly $960 million, and said he was willing to help finance the deal. The hope was that combining two struggling companies would create the economies of scale to remain competitive by cutting costs. A buyout seemed like a long shot to analysts when it was announced, but it shows the scope of the tactics the big chains are willing to consider in order to stay alive.

Competitors and publishers think Bezos is ruthless. He's considered to be a brutal tactician by others in the book publishing industry—book publishers, retailers, and authors, for example—who feel their livelihood is being jeopardized by his cut-rate pricing and arm-twisting to get books at low cost. He seems willing to practically destroy the book publishing industry that got him started if it keeps him ahead.

Is Amazon destroying bookstores? If the big chains are just ailing from a bad economy, Amazon is immune from the recessionary virus. While the chains shrink, Amazon grows. In 2010, Amazon's fourth-quarter revenues grew 36 percent to $12.95 billion, while profits were up 8 percent to $416 million. In that same time period, Barnes & Noble's revenues increased just 7 percent, to $2.3 billion, while its profit fell 25 percent to $61 million. Borders reported a decline in revenues of nearly 18 percent, to $471 million for its third quarter in 2010 (which ended in November) and a loss of $74 million, nearly double its loss from the year earlier. Borders filed for bankruptcy in February 2011.

Of course, Amazon is selling much more than books these days.

But it's still the biggest bookstore on earth. For the third quarter of 2010, it broke out its sales into electronics or media, the latter being primarily books and music. Since Borders and Barnes & Noble also sell music, it's fair to compare their results to Amazon's media revenues in the third quarter. Amazon's media revenues were up 14 percent to $3.35 billion, while Barnes & Noble's revenues dropped 18 percent to $1.9 billion.

The problem the bookstores face is a viciously competitive market. Once it was the big box retailers themselves causing trouble for the independent bookstores. Other retailers—such as Wal-Mart—jumping into the book business have also taken their toll. But everyone knows who's most responsible for a tough bookselling business now. "Today," says Oren Teicher, CEO of the American Booksellers Association, "the competition is clearly coming from Amazon."

And what about investors who decided Amazon would be killed by the chains? Between Amazon's initial stock offering in 1996 and the end of 2010, Barnes & Noble's stock has dropped 29 percent (undulating in between like waves on a Waikiki beach), while Border's stock has fallen 96 percent. Amazon's stock has *risen* 10,320 percent. Based on stock prices at the end of 2010, Barnes & Noble was worth $852 million, Borders was worth $65 million, and Amazon was worth $81 *billion*. That's some very pricey toast.

The main tactic Bezos employs is quite simple: low prices. It's hard to argue with that tactic. Who doesn't want lower prices? It certainly fits in with Bezos's promise to put his customers ahead of others.

But competitors are not happy with Bezos's tactics. "Amazon is a competitor that plays by a whole different set of rules," says the American Booksellers Association's Teicher. Bezos, he says, "does not really care about books. He uses books as loss leaders to sell everything else. He's acquiring customers in order to sell whatever he can ultimately sell them. He has become the expert at marketing [other products] to customers once they've got them on the site."

Furthermore, competitors claim, cheap prices please book lovers in the short term, but may hurt them in the long run. Discounting makes it more difficult for retailers, publishers, and, yes, book authors to make a profit. The more that publishers' profit margins are squeezed, the more focused they become on authors who can make the best-seller lists. The same goes for bookstores that need to move a lot of books to stay in business. "Clearly the deep, deep discounting of both physical and digital books is bad for consumers, publishers, retailers. You end up with fewer choices. The evidence is clear that if you keep discounting the product, there will be less product," says Teicher.

Bezos argues that low prices, combined with new technology, simply broaden the market, lower costs, and enable people to buy more books.

Well, yes and no. Data from Bowker, a company that tracks worldwide book sales from the Books in Print database, indicates that the number of book titles published continues to increase each year. In fact, the number of titles published took a big jump in 2009 (the last year for which it has statistics), increasing 87 percent from 2008, to 1.053 billion. However, a big part of that jump was due to print-on-demand (POD) books, produced by specialty printers that focus on public domain titles, self-publishers, and micro-niche publications. These titles jumped 181 percent over 2008. The problem is that actual sales of these titles are very low compared to books from the major publishing houses.

And retailers say they have not seen the number of readers increase with lower prices. "The big box stores were supposed to increase the numbers of readers too," says Richard Howorth, the owner of Square Books in Oxford, Mississippi, who was one of the teachers of the class on running a bookstore that Bezos took. "But they didn't."

The other complaint is the tactics Amazon uses to keep its prices low. It has enormous influence now, and publishers complain that Amazon puts huge pressure on them to lower wholesale prices, squeezing profit margins. "Amazon dictates terms to publishers," says Howorth.

That means other bookstores, who cannot pressure publishers into giving them similar price cuts, find it hard to compete. A 2003 study by the American Booksellers Association shows that the average gross margins for physical bookstores was 30.8 percent. After payroll, facilities, and other costs were factored in, the result was a net loss of 1.7 percent. For 2009, Howorth's gross sales were up just 2 percent from the previous year.

And then there's the tax issue. Bookstores have to charge sales tax on books. But in 1992, the Supreme Court ruled that online retailers only had to charge sales tax on goods sold in states where they have a physical presence. To Bezos, that means charging tax to buyers in the state of Washington. The lack of taxes in most states means that Amazon's customers get a further price break. That gives Borders and Barnes & Noble a distinct disadvantage for their own online sales, since they have stores in most states. Bookstore owners—and some states—say Amazon should charge tax in any state where it has a distribution center or any other kind of physical presence.

That has led to legal challenges from states and retaliation from Bezos. Texas is a big battleground. In October 2010, the Texas state comptroller sent Amazon a bill for $269 million, the amount the state feels Amazon owes in back taxes, penalties, and interest, because it has a distribution center in Irving. Bezos responded by saying he will shut down the site rather than pay the taxes. This is an unsettled issue that could still cause problems for Amazon in the future, although it will still have an advantage if it limits distribution centers to just a few states.

Retailers are also worried about the pressure Bezos puts on publishers. "The scary thing is that publishers are having such a difficult time," says Howorth. Big retail chains have always put pressure on publishers to discount their books, but Bezos has a very strong arm when it comes to exerting his influence. He has used tactics ranging from temporarily removing a publisher's books from the site to the subtler technique of simply removing the "1-Click" or "Add to shopping cart" icons from their books' listings if they don't give the discounts he requires.

The Authors Guild, an advocacy group for writers, has kept tabs on some of these tactics with a Web site called Who Moved My Button? According to the site, the guild decided to track the events because "publishers are often too fearful of antagonizing Amazon to say anything publicly about such incidents. Authors needn't have that fear (we can keep your identity anonymous), however, and publicity is probably our best collective defense."

From what is known, Amazon's tactic seemed to start in 2008, when Amazon disabled the "Buy" icon from its British Web site for books published by Bloomsbury, and later for books from the British unit of Hachette Livre. The move meant that British buyers could only get the books through Amazon's third-party sellers, not from Amazon directly, and not with Amazon's discounted shipping options. "The buy button is their weapon of choice and that's how they impose market discipline," said Paul Aiken, executive director of the Authors Guild. News of Amazon's disabling of the "Buy" icon went public when Hachette's CEO, Tim Hely Hutchinson, wrote a letter to his authors complaining of the "oddities" of the missing "Buy" icons after he resisted Amazon's demands for lower prices. "Amazon seems each year to go from one publisher to another, making increasing demands in order to achieve richer terms at our expense and sometimes at yours," Mr. Hely Hutchinson said in the letter. "If this continued, it would not be long before Amazon got virtually all of the revenue that is presently shared between author, publisher, retailer, printer and other parties."

Also in 2008, Amazon hit the fastest growing category of new books, print-on-demand (POD), with new restrictions. The self-published authors can sell their books through Amazon, but must print their books through the Amazon subsidiary CreateSpace or those books would lose their "Buy" icons. Bezos promoted it as a cost-saving approach for customers. An open statement on Amazon. com read: "It makes more sense to produce the books on site, saving transportation costs and transportation fuel, and significantly speeding the shipment to our customers and Amazon Prime members. We believe our customer-focused approach helps the entire industry in the long term by selling more books."

But one POD publisher, BookLocker.com, felt it was illegal for Amazon to demand a monopoly in printing POD books. (The majority of such books are sold online, giving Amazon enormous leverage.) BookLocker filed an antitrust suit against Amazon. It was settled in December 2009, with Amazon agreeing not to retaliate against BookLocker for using another publisher, and agreeing to pay BookLocker's legal fees of $300,000. The settlement, however, only applied to BookLocker. Many other POD publishers had already agreed to Amazon's demands.

Perhaps the most surprising trend is that Amazon has not put the small, independent bookstores out of business as everyone once predicted. They were first battered by the big chains and other retailers selling discount books, and the rise of Amazon was supposed to swamp them like little boats hit with the third leg of a perfect storm. But ABA's Teicher says that the small bookstores seem to be learning to weather that storm, although it looked tough for many years. "Between 1994 and 2005, no new stores opened," he says. "There's always churn, but the closing stores weren't being replaced." But things leveled off in 2009. "For the first time in more than 15 years the number of members in the ABA has stabilized," he says. "New stores have opened, and the stores that survived the onslaught are more competitive."

Howorth echoes that view. "What you don't know about Amazon is how much of your business they're taking," he concedes. But, he adds, "I think he's hurting the chains rather than the independents."

It also seems to fit the prediction that Bezos made in 1998, when he promised that Amazon would not destroy the local bookstore. "I still buy half of my books at bookstores," he said. "Sometimes I want the book right now, not tomorrow. Sometimes I just like to get out of the office and go to a nice environment. What you're going to see—and it's happening already—is that physical bookstores will become ever-nicer places to be. They are going to have more sofas, better lattes, nicer people working there. Good bookstores are the community centers of the late 20th century. That's the basis on which they're going to compete. There is plenty of room for everyone."

Well, saying there is "plenty" of room may be a bit of an overstatement. But if the numbers collected by ABA hold up, it may be possible to stay in business. They just have to work at it harder than they ever have before.

Chapter 14

A Cool Guy with a Funny Laugh

The thing about inventing is you have to be both stubborn and flexible, more or less simultaneously. Of course, the hard part is figuring out when to be which!

—Jeff Bezos

Customers loved Amazon.com from the first day they started using it. Industry pundits, who like to demonstrate their expertise on executives and companies, insisted it would never last. In July 1997, Forrester Research President George F. Colony, a respected technology analyst and commentator, said, "Amazon's position is indefensible. They have some nice custom-built software, but that's about all they've got. They don't have a monopoly over the books, and their technology can be duplicated in six months. Forrester Research labeled the company Amazon. toast, while *Barron's* magazine called it Amazon.bomb. Bezos was just another overhyped dot-com rebel without a clue.

It turned out that Amazon's position was highly defensible.

Colony was absolutely correct about what Amazon did not have. But he didn't understand the weapon Amazon did have: Jeff Bezos himself. It's true that, in theory, anybody could have copied Amazon's strategy and reproduced its software. Several executives tried. But imitations of the original are never quite as good, and in the online retailing business, Bezos is a true original.

By now, nobody can dispute that Bezos is a great entrepreneur. His original vision of how the Internet could provide a unique service to customers, as opposed to being simply an online book ordering system, kept Amazon ahead of the competition. Only an entrepreneur with the right vision could see the need for all the features necessary to keep the company ahead, whether he dreamed them up, or his team thought of them first, or he borrowed good ideas from other companies.

Unlike many of the dot-com executives who came later, creating a great company was more important to him than becoming wealthy. Even after the company went public and Bezos was suddenly worth half a billion dollars, he made it a point to let people know he lived in a small apartment in Seattle and drove a Honda (although he later moved into a more impressive house on the border of Lake Washington near the mansion built by Bill Gates and bought three adjacent apartments in Manhattan's art deco Century Building from Sony Music executive Tommy Mottola for $7.7 million).

Perhaps it's his goofy laugh and silly grin that made people underestimate him; certainly his childlike playfulness contributed to that perception. At their wedding reception, Jeff and MacKenzie provided an outdoor adult play area that included water balloons. Even that playfulness served the secondary purpose of helping to draw attention to his company. In 2003, he played tennis with Anna Kournikova at Grand Central Terminal's Vanderbilt Hall in order to publicize the fact that the Anna Kournikova sports bra (designed specially for the tennis star) was making its debut in Amazon's Apparel & Accessories store.

But mostly the skepticism came about because outsiders believed that the much more seasoned executives at the giant bookstore chains were going to outwit him and his "Who needs profits?" strategy. In reality, people just didn't understand him.

That's his own fault. Bezos seems to thrive in the limelight, but he has always carefully controlled his public image. That includes elaborate publicity stunts. In June 1999, in order to celebrate Amazon's ten-millionth customer, Bezos personally delivered a set of golf clubs to a construction worker in Boston while he was at the construction site, with the press in tow. The customer picked, however, was only somewhere around the ten million mark. Bezos chose him because he had to be in Boston anyway at that time. And the clubs he handed to the guy weren't even the ones he ordered. They were just there for the photo opportunity. The customer had to give them back and wait for the real clubs to arrive by mail. These days, Bezos virtually never gives interviews to the press unless he has a specific agenda to promote on the talk show circuit (such as hawking the latest sports bra or Kindle). A CEO who controls his image so carefully may rightly be considered disingenuous, and Bezos is no exception. But he's also farsighted and clever, and manages to get reporters starved for interviews to hang on his every stunt-studded word.

In fact, Bezos personifies a new breed of executive that arose with the emergence of the game-changing technology companies in the 1980s and 1990s. In a January/February 2000 *Harvard Business Review* article by anthropologist and psychoanalyst Michael Maccoby, titled "Narcissistic Leaders: The Incredible Pros, the Inevitable Cons," Bezos was one of the business leaders singled out as a "productive narcissist." (Bill Gates and Larry Ellison also made the list.) These executives have big enough egos to make up seemingly random rules of business leadership. However, unlike other narcissists, they get the job done.

Bezos also has a hugely infectious enthusiasm for his company. One of his incredible talents has been to convince employees, from the highest manager to the lowest customer service rep stuck to her phone ten hours a day, that working at Amazon was not just a job—it was part of a visionary quest, something to give higher meaning to their lives.

To Andreas Weigend, a computer science professor whom Bezos hired in 2002, Bezos is a rock star, partly because of his highly contagious enthusiasm. Weigend describes Bezos as "a cool guy with a funny laugh," and was most impressed with his upbeat and inspiring attitude. "I'm a very positive guy," says Weigend. "And I left every meeting with Jeff more happy, more energetic than when I went in. I had never met anybody who is consistently so empowering."

Bezos is also one of those rare executives who can understand the nuances of technology as well as the big picture of how to succeed. Weigend is a computer scientist, an expert in data mining. He loved the fact that Bezos could understand the technology, and if he didn't, could pick it up easily. Weigend recalls showing Bezos a power-log graph of customers' buying habits on Amazon. It's the kind of graph that turns a trend line showing exponential growth into a straight line for easier analysis. Weigend explained the nuances of the graph to Bezos one day, and a week later Bezos was explaining the graph in a meeting with authority. "After one week, he was talking about it as if he knew it from kindergarten," says Weigend. "That's the wonderful thing about him. He gets it. There's a reason why he's the only CEO from a dot-com company who's still here." That may be a bit of an exaggeration (especially if one considers Google as one of the dot-com companies started in 1999)—but not by much.

Certainly not everybody bought into the Bezos hyperenthusiasm. Former Amazon customer care rep Richard Howard's 1998 article "How I 'escaped' from Amazon.cult" described a cultlike environment in which employees worshipped Bezos as a visionary. They kept talking about Amazon's goal, not to be a gigantic online retailer, but to "change the world." Since Howard had to provide three letters of reference, two writing samples, SAT scores, and college transcripts just in order to get that $10 per hour entry-level job, he assumed there would be ample opportunities for advancement. It turned out to be a job that lasted just a few weeks.

Besides, there was so much enthusiasm from almost everyone around Howard. He noted that he was surrounded by employees who saw Amazon as a "life-changing experience." But Howard never caught the "Amazon Is Great" disease. So many people kept trying to convince him that Amazon was the greatest place on earth, he started wondering if he was, for some reason, being singled out for conversion to the Amazon cult, until he talked to another beginner at the company. Her response: "I've gotten a couple of those too, only my friend warned me in advance that working here was sort of like being in *The Stepford Wives*, so I've more or less taken it in stride."

An article in *The Washington Post* quoted another customer service employee who described the environment as a socialist collective. "It's like Communist China under Mao," the rep said. "You're constantly being pushed to help the collective. If you fail to do this, you're going against your family. But if this is a family, then it belongs on *Jerry Springer*."

In a 1999 article in *The New York Times*, Peter de Jonge explored some of the quirks at Amazon, visiting junior employees and senior managers alike. He also noted the cultlike atmosphere that Bezos inspires—or, at least, projects—about his company. Every manager at the company refused to discuss the company's soaring stock, as though it were an offensive question compared to the company's great vision, and yet all of them seemed to know the current price. "Bezos never serves up e-commerce as naked capitalism," noted de Jonge. "It's 'helping people find and discover the things they want,' 'helping folks make better purchase decisions' and so on and so on. When it comes to seducing his employees, he offers not just a low paying job with a handful of stock options, but also a life's work."

Even in the December 1999 *Time* magazine article that named him "Person of the Year," Bezos was described as "pathologically happy and infectiously enthusiastic." The writer, Joshua Quittner, noted that the company was sprinkled with banners listing Amazon's Six Core Values: "customer obsession, ownership, bias for action, frugality, high hiring bar and innovation"—and dubbed the company culture as "the Cultural Revolution meets Sam Walton," or, more succinctly, "dotcommunism!"

Clearly, the Amazon cult is not for everyone, and those employees who didn't buy it (such as Richard Howard) didn't last long at the company. But many others did, noting that Bezos's enthusi-asm was genuine—and got results. Peri Hartman says that it kept people going when things were difficult. "He was very positive—optimistic is probably a better word. He would say that people will tell you all the time that something can't be done, and if you listen to them, you will fail. He said we will make it work. He saw through all the negativism. It made him fun to deal with."

In Silicon Valley, this cultlike belief in the company is dubbed "the vision thing," and the best CEOs have it (think Steve Jobs). Bezos definitely has it, even if he has been sometimes difficult to deal with on a personal basis. And some of Amazon's most impor-tant employees have found that, like Steve Jobs, he can sometimes be difficult indeed.

Chapter 15

But What Kind
of Manager Is He?

Different executives who have worked with Bezos in the past have strongly different views of his strengths and weaknesses as a manager. He's not always a "nice" CEO. He can inspire and cajole, but can also irritate and berate. He can see the big picture, and micromanage to distraction. He's quirky, brilliant, and demanding. Some of his former employees adore him. Some have found him to have serious shortcomings. All seem to feel that he's a great visionary who knows how to build a lasting company.

"There is no doubt that Jeff is a brilliant businessman with a strong vision for where he wants to take his company," wrote Shel Kaphan, the company's first employee, in an email to me. "However, he is also a demanding micro-manager who is extremely hard to work for. This is one reason there are very few people from the early days of Amazon still at the company. He is also very temperamental, and has (or at least had, when I was there) a bad habit of severely chewing out his subordinates in front of others." Another former executive, for example, said Bezos had an annoying habit of waving his hand in front of subordinates' noses when he didn't want to hear any more of their conversations.

That's part of the hyperactive side of Bezos's personality, one that he sometimes displayed in his previous jobs as well. Although Graciela Chichilnisky, his first employer, considered him an excellent manager, he has always had an enormous amount of energy that might intrude on most associates' comfort zone. "He jumped out at you, his eyes practically jumped out of his sockets," recalls Chichilnisky.

He has always been an unorthodox manager. One former executive recalled that, at an offsite retreat where other managers said the company employees should start communicating more, Bezos stood up and declared, "No, communication is terrible!" He wanted a decentralized, even disorganized company where people could come up with independent ideas rather than subscribe to groupthink. He ruled the company with the "two-pizza team" concept, that dictated any team should be small enough to feed with two pizzas.

Empathy is not something that comes to him naturally. When he was ten years old, on a trip with his grandparents, he decided to try and get his grandmother to quit smoking. For that he relied more on his geekiness than on sensitivity to a sore subject. He calculated that the amount she smoked would reduce her lifespan by nine years. It made her cry. His grandfather had to teach him to be more sympathetic. "My grandfather looked at me, and after a bit of silence he gently and calmly said, 'Jeff, one day you'll understand that it's harder to be kind than clever,'" Bezos said.

He has no empathy for employees who complain about working long hours in pursuit of his quest. Bezos often pushed his people with the finesse of a galley slave driver. One customer service manager recalled that, when the staff got a week and a half behind answering emails despite putting in twelve-hour days, seven days a week, Bezos called her to complain about the lapse. When she told him they couldn't work any harder, he came up with a solution. They dedicated one weekend competing with each other to see who could get through the most emails in the backlogs. During that forty-eight-hour period, everyone worked at least ten hours past their regular shifts. Each person was given a cash bonus of $200 for every thousand messages he or she could answer. It cleared off the backlog.

At other times, Bezos also had a rather geeky way of showing his appreciation for his programmers' hard work, which was often done on their own time. Rather than a raise, he started rewarding exceptional accomplishments with awards named after the Nike slogan "Just Do It." The prize? An old, used Nike shoe. Greg Linden, for example, a programmer who joined Amazon in February 1997, found a better way to parse out similar tastes in books in order to make recommendations to customers. Amazon would recommend books to a customer that were bought by other customers with similar buying patterns. On his blog about his days at Amazon, he recalls that when his program went live on the site, "Jeff Bezos walked into my office and literally bowed before me. On his knees, he chanted, 'I am not worthy, I am not worthy.'" Linden won "Just Do It" awards for this and other accomplishments, and long after losing the shoes, he wrote on his blog, "What was not lost was the sense of pride. I was proud to have gotten that crappy old shoe."

Some former employees also say that Bezos's reputation as a

ruthless business executive is wrong. In an email correspondence with me, Linden describes Bezos as a "geeky, ambitious tinkerer with a focus on doing right for customers (and people in general)." Linden adds that the public perception of Bezos as a hard-charging, take-no-prisoners CEO are incorrect. "I'd disagree with the characterizations of him as competitive (which I think was just misinterpretation of his ambition) or secretive (which I think is more about wanting to protect his team and his customers). Jeff could much more accurately be described as a naively optimistic geek than a calculating megalomaniac."

Bezos also has a lighter side, which, if sometimes goofy, helped to reduce stress. In the very early days, he had employees pick out the twenty strangest titles sold every week, and awarded a prize for the strangest. Some of the winners: *Training Goldfish Using Dolphin Training Techniques*, *How to Start your Own Country*, and *Life Without Friends*. Those are not the kind of titles most bookstores carry regularly. Former programmer Peri Hartman appreciated the silly but upbeat attitude that Bezos embodied like a kid winning a goldfish at a street carnival. Although stressful at times, "Amazon was a fun place to be," says Hartman. "It was stressful in a good way. Jeff has a very positive attitude toward employees."

Hartman also praises Bezos for fostering a sense of camaraderie, noting that there was no infighting between teams vying for attention at Amazon, something that can destroy a young company. The goals, says Hartman, were "innovation, working hard, doing the best job you can. Everybody pulled together to make this happen. You were competing with outside companies, not internally."

Bezos also has the technical chops that allow him to recognize what features could make or break a company. He understands the technology, the problems, and the solutions, and can offer an understanding ear and knowledgeable guidance. But, according to Kaphan, that kind of help didn't always come frequently enough. In the early days, when the company was understaffed and overworked, that meant the programmers had to wing it and hope for the best. "Generally there was enough to worry about that we had to just solve our design problems however we could and move on to the next challenge," says Kaphan. "If anything, there was not enough in the way of design review [from Bezos], which caused some serious problems in the engineering culture of the company, and led to a lot of problems later."

Hartman agrees with both these views. "Jeff didn't do code," he says. "He was the idea guy. He came up with ideas all the time. He probably thought things through more than others." The fact that he focused on the big picture rather than the actual code was still a huge benefit to Amazon, something that Hartman believes "let the company grow into other [new] ideas."

An idea guy can also seem a bit like a king overseeing his kingdom, or perhaps a CEO of a much larger company who can leave the heaviest lifting to his subordinates. In the early days, Bezos did chip in with a lot of mundane tasks, such as packing up books and getting them into the mail for customers.

But he didn't always put in the long hours required of everyone else. Working overtime is not an option for employees at a start-up, it's a mandate. The programmers had to pull many all-nighters in order to meet deadlines. But, frustrating for some, Bezos did not join the late-night work sessions. One former employee says he would "make a show of always getting his eight hours of sleep."

Still, he provided the right kind of guidance from the top, the kind that a CEO absolutely must give. He demanded a robust computer infrastructure, a database management system that could handle orders as the company grew, an ordering system that was easy to use, and the back-end tools that would ensure products could get to customers quickly. Kaphan notes that Bezos paid a lot of attention to the flow of the checkout process and the warehouse order processing software. And everything had to be stable enough, able to handle enough traffic that it would not crash and leave customers stranded, a common problem, especially in the early days of commercializing the Internet. "He was scared to death that we would get all these customers, and then they would go away because the system didn't work well, wasn't easy," says Hartman.

His reputation of being notoriously cheap was very important to him. Not only in hiring and renting office space, but even for the process of furnishing his headquarters. For many years he made a big deal out of the fact that the desks at Amazon were made from doors with legs attached. Other furniture was bought at garage sales and auctions.

In fact, the reputation was sometimes more important to him than the actuality. It's part of Bezos's carefully crafted public image. He made it a point to publicize his early frugality for years, sure to talk about his door-desks in interviews. His personal desk was even featured in a photo shoot in *Vanity Fair*.

The way Jeff put it, the doors represented the company's wisdom in serving the customers rather than the employees. "We have a strong focus on trying to spend money on things that matter to the company and not spend money on us," he said in an interview with a Silicon Valley magazine. "What our furniture looks like does not matter one whit to our customers."

But appearance was even more important than reality. "Sometimes, that meant spending a little bit more to reinforce the idea that we weren't wasting money," said Gina Myers, Amazon.com's first comptroller. "Jeff would say if it looks cheap—even though it's a little bit more expensive—we should buy it because it reinforces our culture of being cheap and not wasting money." Since few customers ever saw the company's furnishings, that perception must have been intended for potential business partners, investors, and the press.

Yes, Jeff Bezos is a showman. Some of his techniques may represent a shoot-from-the-holster approach and, as is always the case with successful start-ups, there was a certain amount of luck involved. As Kaphan noted in his email to me, "Amazon's rapid growth covered over a large number of sins. Given the magnitude of some of the mistakes, I think the company's survival is at least in some significant part due to luck."

But in the end, Bezos's aim was spectacular. Kaphan adds that Bezos fostered a "bias for action. . . . We tried a lot of things and made a lot of mistakes, but managed to avoid any fatal ones." Luck aside, "It also took a lot of intelligence and skill," says Kaphan.

What really made the difference for the company was Bezos's dedication to iteration. He worked at things over and over again until he got it right, at least most of the time. When certain things looked like a lost cause (such as trying to create a search engine to compete with Google), he was willing to drop them. The Kindle, which he considers to be a crucial product for the future, took three years to develop and a couple more to really catch on. Large companies, with businesses to protect and stockholders to please, often have a hard time innovating. "One of the biggest problems with big companies doing clean sheet innovation is that even if you see it, you have to be a really long term thinker, because for a long time it will be a tiny slice of the company," he has said. "The key thing is to be willing to wait 5, 7, 10 years. And most companies aren't willing to wait ten years."

In the end, success makes up for a lot of the pain and frustration that employees might have had to put up with. With that success came an enormously successful IPO, and extraordinary rewards. Bezos showed his appreciation for the work that his early employees did in more ways than one. After the IPO, in order to celebrate Shel Kaphan's fourth anniversary at Amazon.com, Bezos organized a "Shelebration." He chartered a jet to take Kaphan, the engineering staff, and their spouses to Maui for a four-day surprise vacation. When they arrived, Kaphan was greeted by a group of old friends from the Bay Area waiting for him, flown there on a second jet Bezos had chartered just for them.

And that's not even counting the monetary rewards Kaphan received for finally realizing his dream of helping to create a spectacularly successful start-up. Kaphan's hard work netted him over one million shares of stock. When Amazon went public on May 15, 1997, Kaphan suddenly found himself worth over $25 million. At today's prices, depending on how much stock Kaphan has sold over the years, he could be worth over $170 million. Today, Bezos is one of the richest executives in the world. He made number eighteen on *Forbes* magazine's list of the world's wealthiest people in 2010, with a net worth of $12.6 billion.

A hundred million dollars, old mismatched shoes, praise from a prostrate CEO . . . the rewards of working for Jeff Bezos are memorable, often spectacular. It's all part of the unusual world of Bezos. And those were just the early days. Bezos was to prove to be full of surprises in the years to come. The one thing he should never be, however, is underestimated.

Chapter 16

Head in the Clouds

When Netflix streams movies on demand to your home, the programs are sent to you from computers on Amazon. Netflix can't afford (at least not yet) to buy all the computing power needed to load up films instantly and stream them to thousands of customers at any moment. So it rents computers from Amazon's vast store at pennies per minute to handle the tasks, tapping into just as much computer power as it needs at any given moment. It's all part of a surprising business from the online retailing company, called Amazon Web Services, which is part of a larger trend known as cloud computing. Services like this bring in half a billion dollars annually in revenues to Amazon.

Buying companies is a relatively easy way for a stock-rich company to expand its business. But sometimes a great executive will stumble upon an unexpected new idea, or one of his employees may come up with something. The key is the ability to look beyond the current conventional wisdom and embrace a radical new idea. Jeff Bezos has that ability. He doesn't create any structured "skunkworks" organization specifically tasked with the job of creating new businesses, but engineers within the company are given the opportunity to experiment, and good ideas are embraced quickly.

That happened around the turn of the century, even as Amazon seemed to be sinking into the dot-com abyss. Internal tinkering by Amazon engineers led to a new business opportunity that put Amazon at the forefront of cloud computing. Around 2000, some Amazon engineers got the idea of enhancing the Associates and Marketplace programs, which created retail relationships with outside companies and Web sites. What if partners who referred buyers to Amazon also had more access to the rich data and retail software that Amazon had developed? Would that make it easier for other sites to help Amazon sell its wares?

Robert Frederick, then a thirty-one-year-old senior technical manager, was one of the prime developers of the project. He had already created software that could pull out data from Amazon and reformat it to be displayed on the tiny screens of mobile phones and personal digital assistants so that people could browse the site from their mobile devices. Some of his bosses suggested the idea of making similar data available to partners. So Frederick separated the databases holding product information from the software that ran the company and stored passwords and credit card information. That prevented sensitive data from leaking out. Despite some concerns from higher-ups about security, Frederick recalled, "The funny thing is that it did not take a great deal of convincing."

The executives soon realized that they could have a gold mine in their cubicles. By making its data and tools available to outside programmers, Amazon could actually outsource the development of new products—for free. Amazon Web Services was launched

—

in July 2002. "We're putting out a welcome mat for developers," announced Bezos. "This is an important beginning and new direction for us." Developers began creating new sites with original features that could send new buyers to Amazon and help them find and buy products.

One former Amazon developer, for example, created a site that he dubbed "Amazon Light." It included a search box to find any product for sale at Amazon and sported the company's "Buy" button, but added a feature. Search for a DVD, for example, and the site would also tell you if Netflix had the DVD for rent. Look for a CD and the site would also tell you if it was available on Apple's iTunes. Look for a book and the site might even let you know if it was available at your local library.

Again, this is not the kind of thing most CEOs would tolerate. Offer people alternatives to your own store? What was this, the Macy's Santa from *Miracle on 34th Street*? No, but it was a great feature that benefitted customers. Besides, if the customers did decide to buy from the outside site, the transaction actually went through Amazon, which collects a fee for the transaction. Site owners who sent customers to Amazon to buy Amazon products got about a 15 percent cut of any sale they sent to Amazon.

Web services—the process of sharing services between Web sites—had been discussed by Internet pundits for years. Amazon was the first to make the concept a reality in a big way. About two years after the launch of Web services, Amazon boasted sixty-five thousand developers using the program and sending some ten million queries a day to Amazon's servers. That's a lot of new customers.

Further, the offering began to look a lot like the phenomenon now known as cloud computing—tapping into a program sitting on a Web server somewhere rather than one sitting on your own desktop. Another company using the service, for example, Monsoon of Portland, Oregon, offered software that companies could use to tap into Amazon's software to simplify their own inventory management. "Web 1.0 was making the Internet for people; Web 2.0 is making the Internet better for computers," Bezos predicted in a speech at the Web 2.0 conference in San Francisco in 2004. Amazon became known as one of the most innovative companies in cloud computing.

From its initial start in 2002, Amazon Web Services offerings just kept expanding. It can distribute content for other companies (such as Netflix) from its own computers and networks. One of the most important services, EC2, or Elastic Compute Cloud, allows companies to rent exactly as much computing power from Amazon as they need, turning on or off "server instances," a block of specific computer power, within minutes. They pay for instances by the hour, using them to run their own programs without the need to buy their own computers. Amazon can even run a separate computer network for a company's internal communications, and can handle billing and product shipping for other retailers. It's a great way for entrepreneurs to get started without investing in their own computer power, since they can use Amazon's services for pennies a minute, increasing or decreasing the amount of computer power they rent based on their demand at any given time. Some venture capitalists even hand Amazon gift cards to entrepreneurs to help them get started.

That business is growing phenomenally. In 2010, Amazon Web Services brought in about $500 million in revenues to the company. That's less than 2 percent of overall sales. But it has higher

profit margins than the retail businesses—up to 23 percent operating margins compared to 5 percent in the rest of the business.

During the company's shareholder meeting in May 2010, Bezos
saved most of his ever-present enthusiasm for a discussion of
cloud computing services. "It has the potential to be as big as our
retail business," he said. In his opinion, Amazon can do a better job
than most competitors in the business. Cloud computing, he said,
is "a very large area right now [and] it's done in our opinion in a
very inefficient way. Whenever something big is done inefficiently
that creates an opportunity."

That's an astounding claim, since Web Services provides less
than 2 percent of revenues today. But Bezos is now on a 1999-style
rush to build up the business and maintain an early lead advantage. Every day Amazon adds as much computing power as it had
to run its entire business in 2000, when it had revenues of $2.8
billion. It's building specially designed buildings of up to seven
hundred thousand square feet—the size of about sixteen football
fields—to house the computers. And just in case it builds too fast,
in 2010 Bezos introduced Spot Services, which auctions off idle
computing power to other companies at cheaper prices than its
normal rental rate.

Bezos is dreaming up new ways to use that computing power.
His latest move is to lease it not just to companies, but to individuals. On March 29, 2011, he announced Cloud Drive, which allows
people to store their digital files on Amazon's computers through
the Internet. In a move aimed directly at Apple's iTunes (the latest
salvo in an increasing war with Apple and Google), he targeted the
first use at music lovers—although people can use the service to
store any digital information. While Apple and Google waited for

the record labels to decide if they would license music for stream-ing, Bezos decided to take a chance, launch the service first, and ask for permission later. By storing the music online, people can access it from any device. Amazon will charge $20 per year for twenty gigabytes of storage space. (Google charges $5 for the same amount of storage, but not for music files.) Amazon is kick-starting the service by offering up to five gigabytes for free, or twenty giga-bytes for free for one year for anyone who buys an album from its MP3 store.

As of early 2011, Bezos would only say that there are "hun-dreds of thousands" of customers using Amazon Web Services. Wall Street analysts estimate it will be a $750 million business for Amazon in 2011, and $2.5 billion in 2014.

It's hard to imagine a business more distant from retailing than this—except for the fact that Amazon has created such sophisti-cated computer services for itself, so why not offer that power to others for a fee? It's a business that doesn't follow the seasonal ups and downs of retailing, and so provides a more stable revenue stream. And it shows just how bold Bezos can be when adopting new opportunities.

That boldness even extends to a willingness to start competing with some of the companies using his services. In February 2011, for example, Bezos started up Amazon's own video-streaming ser-vice to compete with Netflix. After all, he knows how to do it now (although he's still negotiating with film studios and other video producers to build up his video inventory).

When the Amazon video-streaming service was announced, the stock of Netflix dropped temporarily, then recovered. For now, most industry observers don't feel that Amazon will kill off Netflix. For one thing, Netflix is now in a position to grow in overseas markets before Amazon gets its act together. Also, Netflix customers don't see any need to switch. Investment bank Credit Suisse surveyed over a thousand Amazon customers, and found that four hundred of them were also Netflix subscribers. When that group was asked if they would be likely to drop Netflix for Amazon's service, fewer than 1 percent of them said yes. Most of them thought Netflix provided better value for the money, and liked the fact that they could get both streaming technology and DVDs by mail. This could be an experiment that ends up about as successful as Amazon's earlier attempt to compete with eBay with its own auction service. Unless Amazon can come up with some distinct advantage over Netflix, such as lower prices or better streaming technology, there is no compelling reason to change services. This time, Netflix has the first-mover advantage.

Bezos faced the same obstacle in 2004, when he rolled out Amazon's own search service, called A9. His home-built search algorithms were initially just designed to find products on Amazon's site, while he got a license to use Google's search engine to find items elsewhere on the Internet. Twenty months later Bezos announced his own Web search business to compete with Google. Other Web sites could use A9 to offer search from their own sites, paying only for the storage space or processing power they used on Amazon's computers. That one didn't work out so well, and was later discontinued. Google was just too much of a juggernaut.

Still, Bezos is not likely to ever give up on old-fashioned acquisitions in order to grow his business. He bought another half dozen companies in 2010. His biggest deal was in 2009, when the news spread that Bezos had spent some $1 billion in Amazon stock on a shoe store.

Zappos was founded in 1999 under the name ShoeSite.com. It's known for selling hard-to-find shoes, including vegan shoes (made from artificial leather), but it eventually expanded into other lines: first handbags and purses, then clothing, sunglasses, electronic devices, and DVDs. This looked like a company that might eventually give even Amazon some competition. In 2005, it reached $370 million in revenues, and planned to hit $1 billion revenues by 2010 (a goal it reached in 2008).

But the most important thing about Zappos, and the secret of its success, was its culture. It focused on exemplary customer service and extraordinary treatment of employees. It shipped products to customers for free (even paying return postage if customers decided to send them back), had a one-year return policy, and provided a customer-service call center open twenty-four hours a day. It also paid 100 percent of employees' health care premiums.

How could Bezos resist a company with such ideals and ambitions? In 2005, he visited CEO Tony Hsieh at Zappos headquarters in Henderson, Nevada, to discuss buying the company. Hsieh turned him down, worried that being absorbed into Amazon would destroy the unique Zappos culture. "We told Jeff that we weren't interested in selling at any price," Hsieh wrote in an essay in *Inc.* magazine.

But Bezos returned four years later. Hsieh still didn't want to sell. Zappos was now profitable, but the economy was in a recession, and Bezos was offering an astounding amount of money, although in the form of stock rather than cash. In April 2009, Hsieh flew to Seattle to talk about the company and its culture, including Hsieh's philosophy on "the science of happiness—and how we try to use it to serve our customers and employees better." Bezos suddenly piped up with the question, "Did you know that people are very bad at predicting what will make them happy?" That exact question was the next slide in Hsieh's PowerPoint presentation. From that point on, Hsieh relaxed, feeling that Bezos did understand his dedication to his company's culture: both men were more dedicated to customers than to short-term profits.

They struck a deal on July 20 and closed it on November 1 (at which time the value of the Amazon stock being traded was worth $1.2 billion). The deal included a document "that formally recognizes the uniqueness of Zappos's culture and Amazon's duty to protect it," according to Hsieh. It seems to have worked so far. Hsieh still runs Zappos as an independent subsidiary. In the first quarter of 2010, revenues were up almost 50 percent from the same quarter in 2009.

Of course, it's not certain whether this marriage will remain blissful after the honeymoon. Large acquisitions rarely survive without changing the culture of the acquired company. But there are few executives who would even allow such a crazy culture to continue. Even the board of directors at Zappos just tolerated the philosophy as a social experiment. But Bezos was so excited about this acquisition that he made his own video to discuss it (now available on YouTube).

"Zappos is a company I have long admired for a very important reason," he said in the video. "Zappos has a customer obsession. . . . I get all weak-kneed when I see a customer-obsessed company." In fact, he seems to just love everything about the Zappos culture. "Zappos has a totally unique culture," he added. "I've never seen a company with a culture like Zappos's. . . . That culture and the Zappos brand are huge assets that I value very much, and I want to see those things continue."

Even when not buying companies to add to Amazon, Bezos likes to invest in other companies he believes are exceptional. Despite a lot of bad dot-com investments in the late 1990s, Bezos has not been shy about trying again. He was an early investor in both Google and Twitter. Bezos has learned not only how to create a great company, but how to recognize other great companies in the making. He knows how to pursue his dreams.

And his dreams don't end with Amazon. He has started a second company to try and fulfill a dream he has had since childhood. He wants to explore space.

Chapter 17

Step by Step, Courageously

n 2000, even as Amazon seemed to be falling apart, Bezos started a new business. That was the year he incorporated a company called Blue Origin. But nobody knew about it until *Newsweek* reporter Brad Stone started investigating the name in 2003. It adorned a warehouse on a run-down block along Seattle's Duwamish Waterway. Nobody there would tell him what they were up to, but Stone found information in state databases that revealed it was a space-research company owned by Jeff Bezos.

The first part of the program the firm is pursuing is called New Shepard, a tribute to Alan Shepard, the first American astronaut in space. It is designed to take passengers to the edge of space, and later into orbit, using a propulsion system of peroxide and kerosene. It is destined to become a commercial enterprise, giving space tourists a chance to see the earth and stars from orbit. But its long-term goal, says Stone in his article, is "establishing an enduring human presence in space." It goes back to the dream Bezos presented at his high school valedictorian speech. "We want to try to make it safer and lower-cost for people to go into space," he said in 2003. At that time, the cost of developing this first stage was estimated at $30 million.

Crazy? It's not the first time that adjective has been applied to Bezos as an epithet. But in the age of scaled-back NASA budgets and missions, Bezos is one of a few super-rich entrepreneurs (including Sergey Brin from Google, Elon Musk of Tesla Motors, and Richard Branson of Virgin Atlantic Airways) who are pursuing or funding private alternatives to NASA. Blue Origin is also filled with former NASA engineers and other space scientists.

The company's slogan is the Latin phrase "Gradatim Ferociter," which may be translated as "Step by Step, Courageously." But Internet sites offer translations from "Bit by Bit, Ferociously" to "Step by Step, Arrogantly" to "By Degrees, Fiercely." Any of them might apply to Jeff Bezos.

The first translation is the most likely. On the company's Web site, a note from Bezos explains the company's goals:

> We're working, patiently and step-by-step, to lower the cost of spaceflight so that many people can afford to go and so that we humans can better continue exploring the solar system. Accomplishing this mission will take a long time, and we're working on it methodically. We believe in incremental improvement and in keeping investments at a pace that's sustainable. Slow and steady is the way to achieve results, and we do not kid ourselves into thinking this will get easier as we go along. Smaller, more frequent steps drive a faster rate of learning, help us maintain focus, and give each of us an opportunity to see our latest work fly sooner.

Bezos has also described Blue Origin modestly, as "but a small part of a big, challenging, hard technical effort." His big desire is to make space travel safer and more efficient than anything a big-budget government organization could achieve. The first ship is called *Goddard*, after Robert Hutchings Goddard, an American physicist credited with building the first liquid-fueled rocket in 1926. Goddard was also ridiculed for his grandiose visions of spaceflight.

And Blue Origin is making progress. The first prototype ship, which looks like the cone of a conventional rocket, is designed for vertical takeoff and landing. Vertical landings have never been seriously pursued by NASA, which instead preferred ocean splashdowns or gliding in for a touchdown like the space shuttle. *Goddard*, however, has succeeded in its first test. On November 13, 2006, Bezos, his family, friends, and employees, gathered at the company's launch site in Culberson County in West Texas to witness *Goddard*'s first flight. It took off, rose about 285 feet, then lightly touched down again. Reaching the edge of space will require it to reach an altitude of about sixty-two miles. It's unclear what propellant was used, but it's very clean-burning, without the dramatic blast of fire and smoke that accompanies NASA launches.

Blue Origin publicized the successful launch with a video on the company's Web site (www.blueorigin.com/letter.htm), along with a letter from Bezos. The video seems designed primarily to attract new scientists to the project. The letter starts with the sentence, "Blue Origin wants you!" But be prepared to present your SAT scores and GPA. To further impress viewers, Bezos even sticks an ad in his letter, mentioning that the videos are streamed from Amazon's own Simple Storage Service (S3), which any company can tap into to run its own business.

Then again, the original plans of Blue Origin called for it to begin commercial flights in 2010. In a second test a month later, weather and malfunctions appear to have prevented liftoff.

Nothing more was heard from Blue Origin until early 2010, when NASA awarded it a $3.7 million grant—primarily to design an astronaut escape system and to build a prototype of the rocket for testing on the ground. It was part of a $50 million grant parceled out to five companies (including Boeing) in hopes of starting commercial spaceflight. Then, in 2011, NASA invited eight companies, including Blue Origin, to the Johnson Space Center in Houston to present their proposals for further NASA funding. NASA plans to hand out another $200 million—assuming it gets enough funding from Congress.

The future of spaceflight may indeed be dependent on commercial efforts. If that opportunity arises like bacteria in a petri dish, Bezos wants to be there. If Blue Origin ever turns into a real business, it could even displace Amazon in Bezos's heart and brain. Space exploration, after all, was probably his earliest ambition.

Bezos is applying the same philosophy to Blue Origin as he has to Amazon. The first part of this philosophy is to obsess over customers, in this case creating a comfortable, safe, and exciting service to see the stars.

The second is to invent, and reinvent, tenaciously, until he gets it right. He has enormous faith in his talent for invention. As he explains in a video now available on YouTube, "Whenever we have a problem, we never accept either/or thinking. We try to figure out a solution that gets both things. You can invent your way out of any box if you believe that you can."

Third is to focus on the long term, and Blue Origin will probably be a decades-long project. True, it was easier for Bezos to run Amazon at a loss while the stock was still soaring. The stock crash forced him to pull back for a while to readjust his growth-at-all-costs strategy to one that aimed at a shorter goal of profitability, but he knew that it was time to make that shift in order to assure that Amazon still had a big future. He has always kept his eye on the more distant prize.

The fourth he describes as "It's always Day One." There are always new challenges ahead, new ideas to explore, new directions to turn. As with all great entrepreneurs, his job never becomes mundane or dull. He never thinks of his company as a finished product.

These are extraordinarily simple rules. The only surprising thing about his philosophy is how few executives seem able to follow it. Bezos will stop to rest when he's dead. Until then, he's simply going to keep working, reinventing, trying new things, striving to reach the stars. Someday he may just get there.

Notes

Chapter 1: One Click Is Not Enough

Page

2. **Bezos later told an executive:** Jeff Bezos, "A Bookstore by Any Other Name," speech to Commonwealth Club, July 27, 1998, http://www.commonwealthclub.org/archive/98/98-07bezos-speech.html.

3. **Richard Howard, for example:** Richard Howard, "How I 'Escaped' from Amazon.cult." *Seattle Weekly*, July 15, 1998.

5. **"We're never going to:** Kathy Rebello, "A Literary Hangout—Without the Latte." *BusinessWeek*, June 14, 1997.

5. **"When we do make:** Bezos, "A Bookstore by Any Other Name."

6. **"If publisher X:** David Streitfeld, "Booking the Future; Does Amazon.com Show That Publishing Clicks on the Internet?" *Washington Post*, July 10, 1998.

10. **"People don't just buy:** Bezos, "A Bookstore by Any Other Name."

10. **"To be nine times:** Ibid.

10. **When one elderly woman:** Peter de Jonge, "Riding the Wild, Perilous Waters of Amazon.com," *New York Times*, March 14, 1999.

11. **One of Bezos's:** Bezos, "A Bookstore by Any Other Name."

12. **So what we think:** Ibid.

13. **"probably the most:** R. M. Ballardini, "The Software Patent Thicket: A Matter of Disclosure," (2009) 6:2 SCRIPTed 207, www.law.ed.ac.uk/ahrc/script-ed/vol6-2/ballardini.asp.

14. **one more example:** http://oreilly.com/amazon_patent/amazon_patent .comments.html.

Chapter 2: Portrait of the Entrepreneur as a Young Man

19. **Jeff's family's Texas roots:** Joshua Quittner, "Jeff Bezos: An Eye on the Future," *Time*, December 27, 1999.

20. **"what I considered:** "Interview with Jeff Bezos," *Time*, May 4, 2001.

20. **"One of the things:** Rob Walker, "America's 25 Most Fascinating Entrepreneurs," *Inc.*, April 1, 2004.

20. **"You become really self-sufficient:** Helen Jung, "Amazon's Bezos: Internet's Ultimate Cult Figure," *Seattle Times*, September 19, 1999.

21. **"I've never been curious:** Quittner, "Jeff Bezos: An Eye on the Future."

23. **"I think single-handedly:** Robert Spector, *Amazon.com: Get Big Fast*, HarperCollins, 2000.

23. **A kid who valued:** "Jeff Bezos," CEOBios.com, *Kirby Directory*, June 12, 2010, http://ceobios.com/2010/06/jeff-bezos-amazon-com/.

23. **"I would like to:** Jeffrey P. Bezos interview, Academy of Achievement [no author], May 4, 2001, www.achievement.org/autodoc/page/bezoint-1.

23. **The school now boasts:** www.absoluteastronomy.com/topics/River _Oaks_Elementary_School_(Houston).

25. **One of the stories:** Chip Bayers, "The Inner Bezos," *Wired*, March 1999.

26. **the greatest thinkers:** Academy of Achievement interview.

27. **"He was always:** Bayers, "The Inner Bezos."

27. **"Now the French:** Ibid.

27. **Their venture made:** Sandra Dibble, "'New Pathways of Thought' on Summer Breeze," *Miami Herald*, July 4, 1982.

29. **"The only reason:** Brad Stone, "Amazon Enters the Space Race," *Wired*, July 2003.

29. **"The Effect of Zero Gravity:** Robert D. Hof, "Jeffrey P. Bezos" (in "The E.Biz 25") *BusinessWeek*, September 27, 1999.

29. **"preserve the earth":** Dibble, "Ex-Dropout Leads His Class," *Miami Herald*, June 2, 1982.

30. **I wouldn't mind:** Bayers, "The Inner Bezos."

30. **"One of the great things:** Ibid.

30. *The Miami Herald* **published:** Dibble, "Ex-Dropout Leads His Class."

31. **"I was taking all:** "Interview with Jeff Bezos."

31. **"I always had:** Bayers, "The Inner Bezos."

32. **"I'm not the kind:** Ibid.

Chapter 3: Jeff Gets a Job

33. **"The Universe says:** Spector, *Amazon.com: Get Big Fast.*

33. **"ultimately decided that:** "Interview with Jeff Bezos."

36. **"this was something that:** Spector, *Amazon.com: Get Big Fast.*

36. **"He sees different:** Ibid.

37. **Minor had been building:** Ibid.

37. **"I know you said:** Bayers, "The Inner Bezos."

39. **"the most technologically sophisticated:** James Aley, "Wall Street's King Quant: David Shaw's Secret Formulas Pile Up Money. Now He Wants a Piece of the Net," *Fortune*, February 5, 1996.

39. **"a pleasurable person:** Bayers, "The Inner Bezos."

39. **"Outside of Bill Gates:** Joseph Gallivan, "The Billion-Dollar Bookseller," *Independent*, May 12, 1998.

40. **"The number one criterion:** Bayers, "The Inner Bezos."

41. **"Life's too short:** Ibid.

Chapter 4: Jeff Discovers the Internet

44. **"You know, things just:** "Interview with Jeff Bezos."

44. **"I had never seen:** Bezos, "A Bookstore by Any Other Name."

47. **"Books are incredibly unusual:** Ibid.

47. **with a combined market share:** Spector, *Amazon.com: Get Big Fast.*

50. **"I didn't think of it:** Streitfeld, "Booking the Future"

50. **I knew that when:** Spector, *Amazon.com: Get Big Fast.*

Chapter 5: Three Nerds and an Accountant

58. **A couple of years later:** Spector, *Amazon.com: Get Big Fast.*

58. **(It turns out that story:** de Jonge, "Riding the Wild, Perilous Waters of Amazon.com."

59. **It was apparent that:** Bezos, "A Bookstore by Any Other Name."

60. **"One of the things:** Ibid.

60. **Others at Amazon, however:** Spector, *Amazon.com: Get Big Fast.*

61. **By the end of 1994:** Ibid.

62. **"That's actually a very:** Quittner, "Jeff Bezos: An Eye on the Future."

63. **"I thought he would be:** Spector, *Amazon.com: Get Big Fast.*

Chapter 6: How to Build a Better Bookstore

68. **"We made some good:** Spector, *Amazon.com: Get Big Fast.*

71. **If a book had to be:** Ibid.

72. **They would order books:** Ibid.

73. **About half the customers:** Ibid.

74. **Davis later recalled that:** Ibid.

75. **"The Web is an infant:** Dickson L. Louie, "Amazon.com," paper for Harvard Business School, April 9, 1998.

78. **"They would deliver:** Bezos, "A Bookstore by Any Other Name."

Chapter 7: Growing Pains

82. **One room of the office:** Spector, *Amazon.com: Get Big Fast.*

83. **"Jerry said, 'We think:** Bezos, "A Bookstore by Any Other Name."

83. **"We found that customers:** Video from Jeff Bezos about Amazon and Zappos, July 27, 2009, www.youtube.com/watch?v=-hxX_Q5CnaA,

84. **The employee, Nicholas Lovejoy:** Spector, *Amazon.com: Get Big Fast.*

85. **"It was also a curse:** Bezos, "A Bookstore by Any Other Name."

86. **"I started receiving letters:** Alan Deutschman, "Inside the Mind of Jeff Bezos," *Fast Company*, August 1, 2004.

87. **"I'm an outgoing person:** William C. Taylor, "Who's Writing the Book on Web Business?" *Fast Company*, October 1996.

87. **In the summer of 1996:** Spector, *Amazon.com: Get Big Fast*.

88. **In 1998, Bezos described:** Tim Clark, "Turning to a Global Page," CNET, April 8, 1998, http://news.cnet.com/Turning-to-a-global-page/2009-1082_3-232925.html.

Chapter 8: Money to Burn Through

92. **Although Hanauer was impressed:** Spector, *Amazon.com: Get Big Fast*.

93. **Forget the idea of:** Ibid.

94. **"We're only willing:** Ibid.

95. **"We had to compete:** Michael S. Malone, "John Doerr's Startup Manual," *Fast Company*, February 28, 1997.

95. **"We are not profitable:** Seth Schiesel, "Payoff Still Elusive in Internet Gold Rush," *New York Times*, January 2, 1997.

96. **At a 1997 picnic:** Greg Linden, "Early Amazon: Get Big Fast," Geeking with Greg, January 25, 2006, http://glinden.blogspot.com/2006/01/early-amazon-get-big-fast.html.

96. **"Some people smoke:** Kevin Kelleher and David Lazarus, "Amazon.com High on IPO. So Is Its Valuation," Wired.com, March 26, 1997.

98. **"The site is so fast:** Michael Krantz, "Amazonian Challenge," *Time*, April 14, 1997.

Chapter 9: Growing Up

101. **In the interview, candidates:** "Amazon.com Is Creative When Hiring Employees," *Wall Street Journal*, May 4, 1999.

101. **"One of his mottos:** Bayers, "The Inner Bezos."

101. **Five years after:** "Amazon Is Creative When Hiring Employees."

101. **"We tell the temporary:** Robert D. Hof, "Amazon.com: The Wild World of E-Commerce," *BusinessWeek*, December 3, 1998.

101. **"When you are working:** "Amazon.com Is Creative When Hiring Employees."

104. **"The logistics of distribution:** Anthony Bianco, "Virtual Bookstores Start to Get Real," *BusinessWeek*, October 27, 1997.

105. **There are huge efficiencies:** Ibid.

106. **he searched Amazon's database:** Hof, "Amazon.com: The Wild World Of E-Commerce."

107. **You could say we:** Saul Hansell, "For Amazon, a Holiday Risk: Can It Sell Acres of Everything?" *New York Times*, November 28, 1999.

Chapter 10: Who You Calling a Bookstore?

110. **"Our strategy is to become:** Steve Homer, "Damn! What a Nice, Bookish Tycoon," *Independent*, November 16, 1998.

110. **"We've always said:** Jonathan Rabinovitz, "Page of Progress: Amazon .com's Leader Looks at the Future of Selling on the Internet," *San Jose Mercury News*, October 11, 1998.

111. *The Wall Street Journal:* Suresh Kotha, "Amazon.com: Expanding Beyond Books," October 16, 1998. University of Washington Business School, http://faculty.bschool.washington.edu/skotha/website/cases/Amazon_98.pdf.

111. **"The company has been:** Hof, "Amazon.com: The Wild World of E-commerce."

112. **"This is not a winner-take all:** Jonathan Rabinovitz, "Amazon.com's Leader Looks at the Future of Selling on the Internet," *San Jose Mercury News*, October 11, 1998.

114. **"PlanetAll is the most:** "In Looking to Branch Out, Amazon Goes Out on a Limb," *Wall Street Journal*, May 12, 1998.

114. **"Junglee has assembled:** Ibid.

115. **"Our product extension:** Kotha, "Amazon.com: Expanding Beyond Books."

116. **"Jeff was nervous:** Jodi Mardesich and Marc Gunther, "Is Competition Closing in on Amazon.com?" *Fortune*, November 9, 1999.

116. **"This venture has one:** Ibid.

117. **Bulkeley's job was "to make:** Elisabeth Bumiller, "Public Lives; On-Line Booksellers: A Tale of Two CEOs," *New York Times*, December 8, 1998.

117. **"We're motivated. We've got:** Ibid.

121. **"For all its all-nighters:** de Jonge, "Riding the Wild, Perilous Waters of Amazon.com."

Chapter 11: The Crash

123. **"I'm just plain having fun:** Michael J. Martinez, "Amazon.com Has a Plan, but Jeff Bezos Isn't Revealing What It Is," *Times Daily*, January 30, 2000.

125. **"Membership clubs:** Quittner, "Jeff Bezos: An Eye on the Future."

126. **"We saw the turn:** Katrina Brooker, "Beautiful Dreamer," *Fortune*, December 18, 2000.

127. **"Well, it's never a good:** "Amazon Running Dry?" CBSNews.com, July 28, 2000.

128. **"It's time for these guys:** Nancy Dillon, "Wall St. Tough Sell for Amazon .com," *Daily News*, July 27, 2000.

129. **"We have, for the first:** Brooker, "Beautiful Dreamer."

131. **One analyst estimated:** Melanie Warner, "Can Amazon Be Saved?" *Fortune*, November 26, 2001.

Chapter 12: Bezos Bets Big on the Kindle

135. **"I'm grumpy when:** Onnesha Roychoudhuri, "Books After Amazon," *Boston Review*, November/December 2010.

135. **"You can't ever outbook:** Dan Farber, "Amazon's Jeff Bezos: A Passion for Kindle and Digital Content Delivery," CNET.com, May 28, 2008.

136. **Sometime in 2004:** Gregory Allen Butler, "Kindle: To Change the World," Holistic-Personal-Development.com, November 20, 2007, http://holistic-personal-development.com/2007/11/20/kindle-to-change -the-world/.

136. **One blogger who only:** "What Is Amazon Up to with Lab126?" *Progress Through Unreasonable Behavior* (blog), January 8, 2006, http://uf911 .blogspot.com/2006/01/what-is-amazon-up-to-with-lab126.html.

138. **Google started digitizing:** "Google Editions: A History of Ebooks," *Telegraph*, December 4, 2010.

—

138. **"Consumers have proven:** Jenna Goudreau, "Making Digital Books into Page Turners," *BusinessWeek*, September 3, 2007.

141. **(*TechCrunch* accurately:** Michael Arrington, "Amazon Kindle to Debut on Monday—Ugly but Imressive," *TechCrunch*, November 18, 2007, http://techcrunch.com/2007/11/18/amazon-kindle-to-debut-on-monday/.

141. **"E Ink's technology isn't:** Wade Roush, "Amazon Kindle: One Very Small Step for E-Books," *Xconomy*, November 20, 2007, www.xconomy.com/2007/11/20/amazon-kindle-one-very-small-step-for-e-books/.

143. **(as he wrote in:** John Sargent, "A Message from Macmillan CEO John Sargent," Macmillanspeaks.com, February 3, 2010, http://blog.macmillanspeaks.com/a-message-from-macmillan-ceo-john-sargent/.

146. **John Walkenbach graphed:** John Walkenbach, "Another Kindle 2 Price Reduction," *J-Walk Blog*, October 7, 2009. http://j-walkblog.com/index.php?/weblog/posts/another_kindle_2_price_reduction/.

146. **Bezos smiled and said:** Kevin Kelly, "Free Kindle This November," kk.org, February 2011, www.kk.org/thetechnium/archives/2011/02/free_kindle_thi.php.

146. **He quotes "a reliable:** Michael Arrington, "Amazon Wants to Give a Free Kindle to All Amazon Prime Subscribers," *TechCrunch*, February 12, 2010, http://techcrunch.com/2010/02/12/amazon-wants-to-give-a-free-kindle-to-all-amazon-prime-subscribers/.

Chapter 13: Is Amazon Killing the Bookstore?

149. **Amazon.com is not going to:** William C. Taylor, "Who's Writing the Book on Web Business?" *Fast Company*, October 31, 1996.

154. **Publishers are often too fearful:** http://whomovedmybuybutton.com/aboutus.php.

155. **"The buy button is:** Doreen Carvajal, "Small Publishers Feel Power of Amazon's 'Buy' Button," *New York Times*, June 16, 2008.

156. **"I still buy half of my books:** Taylor, "Who's Writing the Book on Web Business?"

—

Chapter 14: A Cool Guy with a Funny Laugh

159. **The thing about inventing:** Alan Deutschman, "Inside the mind of Jeff Bezos," *Fast Company*, August 1, 2004.

159. **"Amazon's position is indefensible:** Ian Stobie and Wendy Barratt, "Web Forecaster: Forrester Interview," *VNUNet*, July 16, 1997, www.v3 .co.uk/vnunet/analysis/2130440/Web-forecaster-forrester-interview.

160. **At their wedding reception:** Deutschman, "Inside the Mind of Jeff Bezos."

161. **In June 1999, in order to:** Spector, *Amazon.com: Get Big Fast.*

163. **noted that he:** Howard, "How I 'Escaped' from Amazon.cult."

164. **"It's like Communist China:** Mark Leibovich, "Not All Smiles Inside Amazon," *Washington Post*, November 25, 1999.

164. **"Bezos never serves up:** de Jonge, "Riding the Wild, Perilous Waters of Amazon.com."

164. **Even in the December 1999:** Quittner, "Jeff Bezos: An Eye on the Future."

Chapter 15: But What Kind of Manager Is He?

168. **One former executive recalled:** Deutschman, "Inside the Mind of Jeff Bezos."

168. **"My grandfather looked:** Krystal Knapp, "Amazon CEO Urges Princeton Grads to Take a 'Less Safe Path,' *New Jersey Times*, May 31, 2010.

169. **One customer service manager:** Spector, *Amazon.com: Get Big Fast.*

169. **Rather than a raise:** Greg Linden, "Early Amazon: Similarities," *Geeking with Greg* (blog), http://glinden.blogspot.com/2006/03/early-amazon -similarities.html.

172. **"We have a strong focus:** Spector, *Amazon.com: Get Big Fast.*

173. **"Sometimes, that meant spending:** Ibid.

174. **"One of the biggest problems:** Tim O'Reilly, "Jeff Bezos at Wired Disruptive by Design Conference," *O'Reilly Radar* (blog), June 15, 2009, http://radar.oreilly.com/2009/06/jeff-bezos-at-wired-disruptive.html.

Chapter 16: Head in the Clouds

178. **Robert Frederick, then:** Wade Roush, "Amazon: Giving Away the Store," *Technology Review*, January 2005.

184. **Hsieh turned him down:** Tony Hsieh, "Why I Sold Zappos," *Inc.*, June 1, 2010.

185. **But Bezos was so excited:** Video from Jeff Bezos about Amazon and Zappos, July 27, 2009, www.youtube.com/watch?v=-hxX_Q5CnaA.

Chapter 17: Step by Step, Courageously

187. **It adorned a warehouse:** Brad Stone, "Bezos in Space," *Newsweek*, May 5, 2003.

188. **We want to try:** Hof, "Speaking Out: Amazon.com's Jeff Bezos," *BusinessWeek*, August 18–25, 2003.

190. **As he explains in a video:** www.youtube.com/watch?v=-hxX_Q5CnaA

Index

Academy of Achievement, 26
Ackman, William, 150
Advantage Program, 99
Advertising and marketing
  with Internet portals, 99–100
  post-IPO, 99–100
  revenues spent (2009), 100
  word-of-mouth, 10, 83–85
Agency model, 143, 145
Aiken, Paul, 155
Alberg, Tom, 92–93
Alexa Internet, 118, 119–20
Alvarez, Gene, 128
Amazon
  Advantage Program, 99
  advertising and marketing,
    99–100
  Associates Program, 88–90
  best-seller lists, 11
  book reviews by customers, 11,
    86–87

buy button as weapon, 154–55
capitalizing. *see* Financial status
and cloud computing. *see* Amazon
  Web Services
Core Values, 164
development, first phase, 53–65
discounted books, 11, 82, 152
distribution system. *see*
  Warehouses and distribution
as e-commerce site. *see* Amazon
  e-commerce
gifts, 17–18
international expansion,
  115–17, 133
Kindle, 135–47
launch (1995) period, 81–86
legal issues. *see* Lawsuits
location of, 57–60, 81–84
"Look Inside" feature, 12
mission statement, 1
mistakes, early, 83–84

Amazon (*cont.*)
  name of company, rationale for, 59–60, 85
  new features, origin of, 102–3
  number of titles claim, 70, 97
  office space, first, 81–84
  offline compared to online experience, 75–76, 85–87
  online bookstore, idea for, 47–56
  Oracle database, 68
  order handling method, 70–71
  out-of-print books, 8
  pay for access to books, 137
  placement, fees for, 6–7
  print-on-demand (POD) books, 155–56
  privacy issue, 7, 119–20
  publicity, early, 83–85
  recommendations to customers, 7, 12, 87, 118
  sales tax break, 153–54
  "Search Inside" feature, 12
  shipments, first, 84
  shipping times, 71
  as social network, 86
  software system of. *see* Amazon software
  Spotlight, 82, 85
  word-of-mouth about, 10, 83–85
  work environment, 102
  working for. *see* Employees
  See also Bezos, Jeff
Amazon customer service

and Amazon Prime subscribers, 146
  Bezos dedication to, 2–6, 10, 17, 75, 107–8, 185
  consumer-centric approach, 86–87
  goodwill, book reviews as, 86–87
Amazon e-commerce
  Amazon Marketplace, 114–15, 118–19
  Auctions, failure of, 115
  Bezos acquisitions to expand, 113–14, 118
  DVD sales, 113
  logo, change of, 118–19
  music store, 109–12, 118
  privacy issue, 119–20
  products sold, 118, 123, 130, 133
  Visa card offered, 118
Amazon Light, 179
Amazon Marketplace
  and Amazon revenues, 115
  Bezos rationale for, 114–15
Amazon Prime subscribers, 146
Amazon software
  Amazon e-commerce acquisitions, 113–14, 118
  beta-testing site, 77–79
  Bezos as idea person, 171–72
  and browsers, 76–77
  cloud computing, 177–83
  credit card safety, 73–75
  customer information, saving, 77
  early components, 67–79

graphics, minimizing, 78
hypertext, 76
I-Click software, 8–9, 13–16
initial developers. *see*
    Barton-Davis, Paul; Kaphan,
    Sheldon J. "Shel"
inventory tracking system, 71, 103
open-source programs, use of, 69
search capability, 76
Amazon.toast, 96, 159
Amazon Web Services, 177–83
    Amazon Light, 179
    A₉search service, 183
    Cloud Drive, 181–82
    Elastic Compute Cloud (EC2), 180
    growth of (2010), 180–82
    launch of, 178–79
    Netflix use of, 177, 180
    primary task of, 179–80
    Simple Storage Service (S₃), 189
    Spot Services, 181
    video-streaming service, 182–83
American Booksellers Association,
    Bezos in bookselling course,
    1–2, 64–65
Andreessen, Marc, 44, 63
A9search service, 183
Apparel and accessories, 133, 161
Apple Computer
    I-Click licensed by, 15
    iPad as e-book reader, 144
    See also Jobs, Steve
ARPAnet, 21
Arrington, Michael, 146

Ashford.com, 118
Associates Program, 88–90
Auctions
    Amazon, failure of, 115
    Sotheby's, Bezos investment in,
    118
Authors Guild, 154–55

Baker & Taylor, 48–49
Bankers Trust, Bezos at, 35–36
Barnes & Noble
    Borders buyout plan, 150
    as early competition, 47–48
    Express Lane, 14–15
    I-Click patent infringement
        lawsuit, 14–15
    Ingram purchase plan, 104–5, 117
    lawsuits with Amazon, 14–15, 97
    Nook, 144
    online, Bertelsmann purchase,
        116–17
    online launch (1996), 85
    sales growth compared to
        Amazon, 109, 117, 150–51
    stores, closing, 149
Barron's, 159
Barton-Davis, Paul
    background information, 62–63
    and early Amazon, 63–64
    software system, tasks related
        to, 68–69
Bass, Bill, 96
B. Dalton, 149
Benjamin, Keith, 120

Index

Berners-Lee, Tim, 43, 76

Bershad, Brian, 62

Bertelsmann AG

  Barnes & Noble online purchase,
    116–17

  offer to Bezos, 116

Best-seller lists, 11

Bezos, Christina (sister), 22

Bezos, Jackie (mother), 19–23

Bezos, Jeff

  booksellers, strong-arm tactics
    with, 143, 154–55

  in bookselling course, 1–2, 64–65

  business plan for Amazon, 60–61

  and cloud computing, 177–83

  communications networks, early
    work on, 34–39

  companies purchased by, 106,
    113–14, 118, 184–86

  competitors' view of, 150–57

  competition, approach to, 83,
    85–86, 112, 151–52

  and computing, 24, 29–32, 171

  customer service, approach to,
    2–6, 10, 17, 75, 107–8, 185

  education of, 23–32

  employees, interaction with,
    167–71

  entrepreneurial drive of, 20, 23,
    33, 37, 46, 160, 182, 190–91

  expansion of Amazon. see
    Amazon e-commerce; Amazon
    international; Amazon Web
    Services; Blue Origin

  family background, 19–23

  and financial crisis, 124–33

  financing Amazon. see Financial
    status; Profits

  frugality of, 160, 172–73

  growth versus profits strategy,
    95–98, 102, 107–8

  I-Click patent, 9, 13–16

  initial investment in Amazon, 61

  I-Nod patent, 16–17

  Internet, exploration for
    commerce, 43–51

  jobs, first, 27–28, 31–41

  and Kindle, 113, 135–47

  leverage, approach to, 110–12

  managerial style of, 167–75

  mental abilities of, 22–32, 39–40

  mentors, early, 21

  names Amazon, 59–60, 85

  net worth of, 174

  online bookstore, idea for, 47–56

  patent rules, position on, 15

  personality traits, 40, 50, 160–62,
    164–65, 167–74

  as "productive narcissist," 162

  public image, crafting, 161, 172–73

  reading, love of, 24–26

  regret minimization framework
    of, 50–51

  on sales tax, 153–54

  Seattle, move to, 57–60

  shares owned by, 97

  simplicity, dedication to, 8–10

  software, early components, 67–79

space exploration, interest in, 29–30, 187–91

as *Time* Person of the Year, 121

wife. *see* Bezos, MacKenzie Tuttle

women, efforts to meet, 40–41

and Zappos, 184–86

See also entries under Amazon

Bezos, MacKenzie Tuttle

and early Amazon, 64

meets Jeff, 41

move to Seattle, 58–60

wedding, 160

Bezos, Mark (brother), 22

Bezos, Miguel (Mike) (father), 22

investment in Amazon, 61

Bibliofind, 118

Blodget, Henry, 120

Blue Mountain, 118

Blue Origin, 29, 187–91

company slogan, 188

goals of, 188–89

Goddard launch, 189–90

NASA grant to, 190

BookLocker.com, 155–56

Book publishing

Bezos strong-arm tactics with, 143, 154–55

discounted books, impact on, 152–53

print-on-demand (POD) books, 152

titles published, increase in, 152

Book reviews by customers, 11, 86–87

Booksellers

Amazon's impact on, 150–57

loss leaders, 82

mail order, 48

offline compared to online experience, 75–76, 85–87

pre-Amazon facts about, 47–50

sales tax on books, 153–54

small, survival of, 156–57

specialty companies, 48

superstores, 47–48

See also Barnes & Noble; Borders

Books in Print, 71, 152

Borders

Barnes & Noble buyout plan by, 150

as early competition, 47–48

losses (2010), 149–50

BountyQuest, 15

Bowker, R. R., 71–72, 152

Bradbury, Ray, 33

Brand, Stewart, 56

Brannon, Kelyn, 126

Branson, Richard, 188

Brin, Sergey, 9, 45, 188

Browsers

Amazon's operation with, 76–77

early browsers, 43–44, 63, 77

BTWorld, 35–36

Bulkeley, Jonathan, 117

Buy button, as weapon, 154–55

Cadabra, Inc., 59

Calveley, Peter, 15–16

Canada, Amazon's expansion, 133

CC Motel, 73–74

CDNow, 110, 112

CDs, Amazon's expansion, 109–12, 118

Chichilnisky, E. J., 32

Chichilnisky, Graciela, 32, 34–35, 39, 168

Circuit City, 132

Cloud computing. See Amazon Web Services

Cloud Drive, 181–82

CNET news service, 37

Cohen, Jonathan, 110

Colony, George F., 159–60

Competition
  Amazon Marketplace, use by, 114–15
  to Amazon music store, 110
  Barnes & Noble. see Barnes & Noble
  Bezos, negative views by, 150–57
  Bezos approach to, 83, 85–86, 112, 151–52
  Bezos growth strategy against, 95–98, 102
  from distributors, 104–5
  growth versus profits strategy, 107–8
  to Kindle, 144–45
  video-streaming services, 182–83

Core Values, 164

CreateSpace, 155

Credit card transactions, early system, 73–75

Crown Books, 49

Customer service. See Amazon customer service

Cybook, 138

Davis, Paul. See Barton-Davis, Paul

DBM manager, 69

De Jonge, Peter, 121, 164

Della & James, 118

D. E. Shaw
  Bezos at, 37–45, 50–51
  Internet companies of, 45

Digicash, 16

Digital Book, Inc., 138

Dillon, Eric, 92–94

Discounted books
  and Amazon, 11, 82, 152
  impact on book industry, 152–53

Disney, Walt, 26

Distributors
  drop-shipping, 104, 105
  and early Amazon, 87–88
  online business, failure of, 104–5
  of wholesale books, 48
  See also Warehouses and distribution

Doerr, John, 44, 94–97

Dot-com companies. See Internet companies

DREAM Institute, 27–28

Drugstore.com, 106, 118

DVDs, Amazon sale of, 113

Dynabook, 137

Early adopters, 83–85

E-bay, versus Amazon Auctions, 115

E-books
  agency model, 143, 145
  and Amazon. *see* Kindle
  devices, competitive, 144–45
  early readers, 137–38
  free, 147
  future view for, 146–47
  Google, 144–45
  market, growth of, 142, 144
  pricing of, 142–43

Edison, Thomas, 26

E Ink Corporation, 140

Elastic Compute Cloud (EC2), 180

Electronics, 118

Ellison, Larry, 162

Employees
  Bezos interaction with, 162,
    167–71
  compensation, 101
  and cult of Amazon, 163–65
  expansion (1998), 109
  firing (2000), 126, 129, 131
  hiring practices, 100–102
  individualistic, 101–2
  "Just Do It" award, 169
  two-pizza teams, 168
  Wal-Mart executives, hiring of,
    106–7
  work environment, 102

Endurance (Lansing), 11

E-Niche, 118

Equinet, 34–35

Erwise, 76

Everybook, 138

Express Lane, 14–15

Farsight, 45

Financial status, 91–98
  cost-cutting, 129–31
  decline (2000), 124–29
  first investors, 61
  growth versus profits strategy,
    95–98, 102, 107–8, 125
  investment advisors, 93
  IPO, Amazon, 96–97
  leverage, Bezos approach to,
    110–12
  losses and debt (1999), 124
  pro forma net profit (2002), 132–33
  raising capital, problems of, 92
  recovery of Amazon, 128–33, 150
  revenues in 2010, 150–51
  share price, growth rate, 61,
    96–97, 120–21, 131, 133, 150
  stock downgraded, 128, 130
  valuations of Amazon, initial,
    92–97
  Web site building, profitability of,
    131–32

Fitel, Bezos at, 32–35

Food and grocery items, 118

Fortune, 126, 129

Frederick, Robert, 178

Free Software Foundation, 14–15

Frisbee, 13

Frox, Inc., 55

Galli, Joseph, 123, 126–27
Gates, Bill, 45, 61, 160, 162
Gear.com, 118
General Atlantic, 93–94
Germany, Bertelsmann offer, 116–17
Gifts
    Conversion Rules Wizard, 17–18
    returned, cost of, 18
Gise, Lawrence Preston
        (grandfather), 20–21
Goddard, 189–90
Goddard, Robert Hutchings, 189
Gold Box, 102
Google
    digitized books, 138, 144–45
    e-books, 144–45
    graphics, minimizing, 78
    News, linking to source, 90
    privacy issue, 120
    and simplicity, 9
Graphics, and site speed, 78

Hall, Colonel Robert, 19
Hanauer, Nicholas J., 57–58, 60
    as investment advisor, 92–93
HarperCollins, 138
Hart, Michael, 137–38
Hartman, Peri, 8–9, 100, 165, 170
Heal, Geoffrey, 34–35
Hiring, interview process, 100–102
Hirsch, Harvey, 36
HomeGrocer.com, 118
Home improvement products, 118
Howorth, Richard, 153–54

on cult of Amazon, 163
on customer service, 1–2
and early Amazon, 3–4
meets Jeff, 1–4, 64–65
Hsieh, Tony, 184–86
Hutchinson, Tim Hely, 155
Hypertext, Amazon's system, 76

IBM, Bezos at, 31–32
Infinity Cube, 25
Ingram, John, 50
Ingram Book Group, 48–50, 57
    Barnes & Nobel purchase plan,
        104–5, 117
    online business, failure of, 104–5
Ink, electronic, 140–41, 145
I-Nod patent, 16–17
International expansion,
        115–17, 133
Internet
    browsers, first, 43–44, 63
    and commerce, early possibilities,
        43–51
    development of, 21
    dot-com fever, 93
    growth rate, 44–45
Internet companies
    Amazon as success, 60
    dot-com collapse, 98, 124
    employees, talent versus
        experience, 63–64
    venture capital method, 61
Internet Movie Database
        (IMDb), 113

Inventory tracking, Amazon's system, 71, 103
iPad, 144
IPO, Amazon, 96–97
iPod, 138
ISBN, and database creation, 48–49, 71–72
iTunes, 112, 135

Jay, Alan, 113
Jobs, Steve, 165
  e-books, agency model, 143
  online music, 112, 135
Jorgensen, Jacklyn Gise. See Bezos, Jackie (mother)
Junglee, 114
Juno, 45
"Just Do It" award, 169

Kaleida Labs, 55
Kamala, 102
Kaphan, Sheldon J. "Shel"
  background information, 54–55
  on Bezos, 167, 173
  and early Amazon, 55–59
  meets Bezos, 55–56
  net worth of, 174
  software system, tasks related to, 68–69
Kay, Alan, 137
Kelly, Kevin, 146
Kindle, 135–47
  Bezos introduces, 139
  Bezos on, 135

  books, cost approach, 142–43
  cost-cutting, 146
  development of, 136–37, 173
  ease of use, 140
  electronic paper/ink, 140–41, 145
  and future of e-books, 146–47
  initial sales, 139
  inspiration for, 113, 135
  negative factors, 141–42
  versus physical books, 134, 137
  pre-Kindle devices, 137–38
  self-published, royalties to, 144
Kournikova, Anna, 161
KPCB (Kleiner Perkins Caugield & Byers), 94–97

Lab126, 136–37, 140
Laventhol, Peter, 54, 55
Lawsuits
  and Barnes & Noble, 14–15, 97
  BookLocker antitrust suit, 155–56
  sales tax issues, 154
  and Toys "R" Us, 132
  and Wal-Mart, 106–7
Lazy G ranch, 19–20
Leather goods, 118
Leverage, Bezos approach to, 110–12
Linden, Greg, 67, 102–3, 169–70
LinkedIn, 53–54
Local booksellers, survival of, 156–57
"Look Inside" feature, 12
Lovejoy, Nicholas, 84, 101
Lucid, Inc., 54–55
Lynx, 76

Maccoby, Michael, 162
Macmillan, 143
Merrill Lynch, 37
Miami Palmetto Senior High
     School, 26–27
Microsoft Internet Explorer, 77
Microsoft Reader, 138
Microsoft Sidewalk sites, 89
Middelhoff, Thomas, 116–17
Minor, Halsey, 37, 39–40
Morrison, Toni, 41
Morrison, Walter Frederick, 13
Mosaic, 43–44, 63, 77
Mottola, Tommy, 160
Movement recognition, I-Nod
     patent, 16–17
Movies
     DVDs, Amazon sale of, 113
     Netflix, 177, 180, 182–83
     streaming by Amazon, 182–83
Murdoch, Rupert, 90
Music
     Amazon's expansion with,
          109–12, 118
     Cloud Drive file storage,
          181–82
     competition, online, 110
     iTunes, 112, 135
MusicFind, 118
Musk, Elon, 188
Myers, Gina, 173

n2k, 110
NASA, grant to Blue Origin, 190

Netflix, 177, 180
     Amazon as competitor, 182–83
Netscape, 44, 63, 77, 93, 98
News Corporation, 90
Newsweek, 187
New York Times, The, 100, 164
Next-Card, Inc., 118
Nook, 144

Office products, 133
I-Click software
     Apple licensing of, 15
     challenges to, 13–16
     development of, 8–9
     patent infringement, Barnes &
          Noble, 14–15
     patent protection, 9, 13–16
Open-source programs, Amazon's
     use of, 69
Oracle database, 68
Ordering, with one click. see I-Click
     software
O'Reilly, Tim, 13–14
Out-of-print books
     Amazon's offering, 8
     Bibliofind, Bezos purchase, 118
     order handling method, 71

Page, Larry, 9, 45
Patents
     for Associates Program, 88–89
     I-Click software, 9, 13–16
     process patents, 9
PlanetAll, 7, 113–14

Princeton University, 30–32
Print-on-demand (POD) books
    market for, 152
    printing, Bezos demands of,
        155–56
Privacy
    issues with Amazon, 7, 119–20
    issues with Google, 120
Profits
    and Amazon retailing, 110
    versus growth strategy, 95–98,
        102, 107–8, 125
    losses and debt (1999), 120–21,
        124, 128
    recovery of Amazon, 128–33
Project Gutenberg, 138

Quadrangle Club, 32
Quittner, Joshua, 164

Raghavendran, Ramanan, 93
Random House, 116, 138
Rare books, Bibliofind, Bezos
        purchase, 118
Ray, Julie, 24–25
Recommendations to customers,
        12, 87
    data collection/privacy issue, 7,
        119–20
    expansion of capability, 118
Risher, David, 32
River Oaks Elementary School, 23–24
RocketBook, 138
Rowen, Mark, 127

Sales tax on books, 153–54
Sargent, John, 143
Sawyer, Ryan, 102
ScenicSoft, Inc., 62
Search, A₉search service, 183
"Search Inside" feature, 12
Seattle, Washington
    Bezos selection for Amazon, 57–60
    office space, first, 81–84, 172
Self-published authors, royalties
        to, 144
Share price. See Financial status
Shaw, David
    background information, 38–39
    Bezos work with, 37–45, 50–51
Shepard, Alan, 187
Shipping times, 71
Shopping comparison software, 114
Sidewalk sites, 89
Silver Knight science competition, 29
Simple Storage Service (S₃), 189
Slade, Jane, 101
Social networks, Amazon as, 86
SoftBook, 138
Sony Reader, 138–39, 144
    e-ink technology, 141
    limitations of, 139
Sotheby's, 118
Space exploration
    Bezos early interest in, 29–30
    private alternatives, 188
    See also Blue Origin
Spector, Robert, 70
Sporting goods, 118

Index

Spotlight, 82, 85

Spot Services, 181

Stone, Brad, 187

Strait, George, 20

Strait, Mattie Louise
(grandmother), 20

Student Science Training
Program, 29

Tarbert, Todd, 59

Tax, sales tax on books, 153–54

Teams, two-pizza, 168

Teicher, Oren, 145, 151–52

Testing of Luther Albright, The
(Mackenzie book, Bezos), 41

Ticketmaster, 89

Time, 98, 121

Tool Crib, 123

Toys and games, 118, 131–32

Toys "R" Us
lawsuit against Amazon, 132
Web site building project, 131–32

Tuttle, MacKenzie. *See* Bezos,
MacKenzie Tuttle

United Kingdom
Amazon expansion, 115
buy button, use of, 154–55

UNIX, 69

USPAN, 62

USWeb/CKS, 99–100

VerticalNet, 127

Vesper, Bernard, 19

Video-streaming. *See* Movies

ViolaWWW, 76

Visa, Amazon card, 118

Walkenbach, John, 146

Wall Street Journal, The, 85, 100, 110

Wal-Mart
as bookseller, 151
lawsuit with Amazon, 106–7

Walton, Sam, 107

Warehouses and distribution, 106–8
and Amazon losses, 125
computerized system, 107
initial expansion, 103–4
Wal-Mart lawsuit, 106–7

Washington Post, The 164

Wedding gift registry, 118

Weigend, Andreas, 162–63

Weinstein, Joshua, 27

Werner, Rudolf, 29–30

Werner, Ursula "Uschi," 27–28

Whole Earth Truck Store, 56

Who Moved My Button, 154

Wilson, Evan, 138–39

World Wide Web, 43, 63, 76

Yahoo What's Cool, Amazon on, 83

Yang, Jerry, 83

Zappos, Bezos purchase of, 184–86

Zehr, Gregg, 136–37

zShops
Amazon Marketplace, 114–15,
118–19